ANDY FORDHAM
THE VIKING

with Humfrey Hunter

JOHN BLAKE

Published by John Blake Publishing Ltd,
3 Bramber Court, 2 Bramber Road,
London W14 9PB, England

www.johnblakepublishing.co.uk

www.facebook.com/Johnblakepub   facebook

twitter.com/johnblakepub   twitter

First published in paperback in 2012

ISBN: 978-1-85782-813-9

British Library Cataloguing-in-Publication Data:

A catalogue record for this book is available from the British Library.

Design by www.envydesign.co.uk

Printed and bound in Great Britain by CPI Group (UK) Ltd

1 3 5 7 9 10 8 6 4 2

Papers used by John Blake Publishing are natural, recyclable
products made from wood grown in sustainable forests.
The manufacturing processes conform to the environmental
regulations of the country of origin.

Every attempt has been made to contact the relevant copyright-holders,
but some were unobtainable. We would be grateful if the
appropriate people could contact us.

CONTENTS

For Jenny, Raymond and Emily,

and in memory of Peter Stanlick,
a friend I will miss forever.

ACKNOWLEDGEMENTS

I've got so many people to thank I'd fill another book if I mentioned them all, so I've tried to keep this as short as possible. (It might not look like that, but I really have!) All these people have helped me in some way, whether it was supporting me when I was at my lowest point, helping me in the early stages of my darts career, or even just making me laugh:

My mum and dad, who have done so much for us and my brother and sisters – John, Julie and Tracy. Jenny's dad, who has done the same for her and her sisters – Sally, Wendy and Mandy.

My kids, Raymond and Emily, who have been through so much over the years. I'm so proud of the strong, brave adults you have become. You two mean the world to me.

I have no idea of how many doctors and nurses have looked after Jenny and me. But I do know that without you neither of us would be here now. You all do an amazing job and I owe you so very, very much.

Stubbsy and the Goalie (Ray Stubbs and Andy Goram) – you've been brilliant.

My manager, Steve Mottershead – thanks for everything you've done for me.

Cass Pennant, Paul Woods and Philomena Muinzer at Pennant Books – for giving me the opportunity to do this book.

Humfrey Hunter – for putting the story together.

A very special big thank-you to everyone at my sponsor, Winmau, who make the best darts and dartboards in the world!

I'd also like to single out the following:

Graham Fry and Nick Loizou from IMG; Ollie Croft, Sam and Marie Hawkins, Alan and Gloria Robson from the BDO; Roger Nixon; Gary Davies; Kenny Tarr; the Angerstein football team (I won't mention any names in case the police are looking for them); Dave 'the Greek' Ahmet; Dave Stevenson (Stevo); Chocolate; John O'Connor; John Bassett; the Erith darts team (Phil Brooker and Ian 'Crust' Covil); Jim and Sadie Duncan; Jeff and Anne Wylie; Barry Hearn and his gang at the PDC (Matt and Andy); James from Sky, and everyone else involved in 'The Showdown'; Jason Thame; Andy Jenkins; Colin Monk; 'Yellow Pages'; James Wade; Frank Wooder; David Croft from the BBC; Mark Williams (I don't know why!); Captain Walsh (thanks for 2004); Robert and Sylvia Holmes; Dave and Vi Alderman; Daryl Fitton and Christal; Tony and Gill O'Shea; Eric Bristow and Phil Taylor for the foreword and introduction to this book; Tim Andrews; Gary Robson; Ian and Joan Waller; special thanks to Martin and Bridie Feeney; Tiger Carroll; Owen King; Hotels.nl – Kees, thank you for your faith in me; my good friend Gary Blade, who lives in Tenerife, my second home (long live Status Quo!); Craig, Mary and Campbell; all at the

ACKNOWLEDGEMENTS

Bluebell in Tenerife; Lenny 'Boris' Daniels (the worst driver ever). And all my mates who have watched and supported me over the years – particularly Carl Wilkins, who earned me my nickname when he came to watch me in the 1995 World Championships wearing a full Viking outfit.

I love going to Holland and would like to mention a few people who have helped make my time there so enjoyable:

Appie and Angelique; Big Frank Penders; Jeroen Heubach of FC Twente; the Dutch darts federation; and the Dutch people in general, for being so friendly and welcoming.

I'd also like to acknowledge some friends who are sadly no longer with us: Lorna Croft; George Noble Sr.; Alan Bailey; Peter Dean; Lou 'the Shoe' Shannon (the strangest team manager I have ever had); Norman McAdams (a gentleman); Jim Granahan; Duncan Frame; and Peter Stanlick – may you all rest in peace.

Finally, to Jenny – you're everything to me. Thank you for saving my life.

Andy Fordham

FOREWORD

Andy is a lovely guy, but as a drinker he was an animal. He pressed the self-destruct button with booze and could easily have killed himself. With the way he lived his life, winning the World Championship was just about the worst thing that could have happened to him, because when you win it everyone's so nice to you. You get everything free and they kill you with kindness.

Andy just couldn't say no to the drink and it nearly did for him. I'm glad he survived and is doing well now.

Eric Bristow – five times World Darts Champion

INTRODUCTION

Andy Fordham is a gentle giant and one of the nicest guys in darts. We have played each other a couple of times, most memorably when we played our head-to-head in 2004, at the Circus Tavern in Purfleet. That night was a sign of things to come for Andy. I recall vividly the feelings of dread I had when he told me he couldn't breathe properly and would have to pull out. It was so hot on the stage that night and the crowd were so close that it made the atmosphere white-hot.

Andy will be the first to admit that his problems were self-inflicted. I'd certainly never condone the lifestyle he had, but I'm so pleased that he's managed to change his life around. He has virtually come back from the dead to get a second chance in life. I hope he can get back to playing darts at the highest level possible. His switch to the Professional Darts Championship this year certainly shows that he has the courage and determination to try and make that happen. I wish him well.

Phil 'The Power' Taylor – twelve times World Darts Champion

PROLOGUE

Sunday January 11th 2004
The British Darts Organisation World
Championship Final

'Ladies and gentlemen, let's play darts! Will you please welcome "The Viking" – Andy Fordham!'

Martin Fitzmaurice introduced me as I walked out onto the stage, with 'I'm Too Sexy' by Right Said Fred blasting out behind me. The crowd went wild. I'd never had a reception like that before and I couldn't wipe the smile off my face. I waved back and they cheered even more. I felt good, relaxed and ready for the biggest game of my life.

Next it was my opponent's turn to make his entrance.

'Please be upstanding for royalty. Ladies and gentlemen, "The King" – Mervyn King!'

Out came Merv, accompanied by Robbie Williams's 'Let Me Entertain You'. We shook hands, wished each other luck and waited for the crowd to stop cheering so we could start the game.

I was trying my best to stay calm and focused but my mind was racing. Suddenly I wasn't sure if deserved to be there. I worried that I'd fluked my semi-final win. Maybe I wasn't actually one of the two best players in the world, after all? Maybe I was about to be humiliated, beaten out of sight by a much better player?

No, don't be stupid, I told myself. *You're here because you're good enough to win. Think positive – you could be World Champion in a couple of hours, your dream could come true. Don't think about how you'll feel if you lose.*

But I couldn't shake off that nagging question: if I lost tonight, would I ever get the chance to win it again?

There were too many unanswerables bouncing around my brain, so I thought about the facts instead. But that didn't help. Merv was higher than me in the world rankings, but the bookies had us both at 5/6 to win. It couldn't have been any closer.

Even the omens had us level. Merv had beaten Ritchie Davies in the semi-final, and Ritchie had lost to the previous three World Champions in the run-up to their titles – so that meant Merv was going to beat me. But then, Merv had also lost to the same three World Championship winners in the last three tournaments – so that meant *I* was going to beat *him*.

I didn't pay any attention to either scenario. How can something that happened last year affect what goes on twelve months later?

It can't. Only me and Merv could decide who'd be the winner.

I thought I had a good chance. I'd come through a close semi-final against Ray Barneveld, one of the best players in history, and felt ready for the next challenge. He'd been odds-on to beat me, but I'd won.

PROLOGUE

Even though I'd beaten the tournament favourite in my last game, most of the other players fancied Merv. (In fact, John Walton was the only one I know of who predicted I'd win.) But their opinions didn't bother me.

I've never cared who's favourite and who isn't. I always see my next match as just another game and give every opponent the same level of respect, no matter who they are. Then I go out there and play my game as well as I can.

I can't control what the other guy does, so there's no point worrying about it. I respected Merv, but I wasn't afraid of him – not even with a World Championship at stake.

The crowd went quiet. It was game time.

'The very best of order, please. Andy to throw first . . .'

ONE

THE PEAK

I was about to throw my first darts in a World Championship Final. The biggest three shots of my career.

So what did I score? Five, 20 and five, for a grand total of 30 – not quite the start I'd hoped for, after averaging well over 90 per three darts through the tournament.

Oh well, I told myself, *it can't get any worse.*

Merv hit 140. Given that you have to score 501 to win a leg, this meant I was behind already. The advantage of throwing first was lost. But it was still only the first leg, and a darts match is a marathon – not a sprint. This one was the first of six sets and each set is the first of three legs, so there was plenty of time left.

I picked my game up a little bit after that first stutter, but Merv still easily won the leg. He finished on a double 16, which he hit first time – a good sign for him. You have to finish every leg with a double – one of the beds in the outer ring of the board – or on the bullseye in the middle, both of

1

which are the most important throws in the game. This makes them the hardest, too, and the easiest to miss.

Merv was hitting his already, good news for him but not for me. He opened the second leg with a 140 and I came back with 60, so I was behind again straight away. He won this leg even more easily, I was still on 274 when he finished. We'd played only once before, in the World Championships during the first round in 1999; I'd won that game. This time round it didn't look so promising.

Shortly after we started throwing, a photographer at the side of the stage started taking photos. The clicking noise as I was standing on the oche started annoying me. I tried to ignore it, but realised I wasn't going to be able to shut it out before it really started putting me off.

I said something to the referee and he asked the guy to stop. I'd never had to do anything like that before. I felt a bit out of order, asking him to stop doing his job, but he didn't seem to mind too much.

With that now out of the way, I tried to be as cool as possible and relaxed a bit. I watch that moment on telly now and I can see how focused I looked. I can't believe I seemed so calm in that situation. I certainly didn't feel like that inside.

My darts improved immediately. I opened the third leg with a maximum – three treble 20's to make 180 – the first of the match. That 180 signalled to everyone there – especially me – that I could handle it. I was in the World Championship Final and had thrown a maximum. I was on my way.

Throwing your first 180 is an important moment in a game. A leg in darts is basically a race between the players from 501 to zero. The tactics are simple: when you throw first in a leg you want to score heavily early, so that your opponent feels under pressure to come up with big scores in order to keep up with you. If you can score heavily early a few times and win the legs, your opponent will get used to the feeling of playing miles behind you when he's throwing second. That means you reduce the chances of losing one against the darts.

It's the same idea as tennis players desperately wanting to hold their serve, so that they have a solid base to attack the other player on his. In darts, it's all about putting pressure on your opponent by scoring heavily.

Darts isn't a complicated game. Most matches are won by the guy who holds it together better, and it's a bit like golf in that respect. All the players are capable of hitting 180's every time they throw, but only the truly great ones do it when the pressure is on, when it really matters.

To me, Eric Bristow is the greatest of them all and my personal hero. In the 1980 final, when Eric beat Bobby George, Bristow was four-three up and one set away from winning the match (they played best of nine in those days, so it was the first to five). It was two-two in legs and, after Eric wobbled in the middle of the leg and missed a shot at 120 for the Championship, Bobby only had to get 18 with three darts to make it four-four in sets, with the decider to follow.

He went for a double nine but missed, and so had nine left. Because you have to finish on a double, Bobby went for a single one to leave himself a double four. But he missed it and put it in the 20 bed instead, which meant his score was scratched, he was back on 18 and it was Bristow's chance to throw for the title. It was an unbelievable miss, the darts equivalent of a top footballer missing an open goal from two yards out. After that, Bobby turned round, walked back and put his darts in his top pocket. He gave up. In that second he knew he'd lost.

In his book, *The Crafty Cockney*, Bristow says, 'I couldn't believe . . . he'd missed a single number. No good darts player ever misses a single number, especially one playing in the World Final. The pressure had got to him. He put his darts back in his top pocket before I'd even checked out, a signal that he knew it was over.'

That's what it takes to win close games – you have to be able to handle the pressure. Eric could, but Bobby couldn't – despite being one of the best known faces in the game, he would never win a World Championship. Bristow won five and, with Phil Taylor, is one of the two highest ranked ever. The end of that leg against Bobby George showed exactly why that is.

I desperately wanted to follow in my hero's footsteps as World Champion. This was my chance. After my 180, Merv came back with 44 and I was back in the game. All it takes is one decent throw for you to relax and start playing properly.

I thought that would be my moment, but it wasn't quite that simple. (In darts, it never is – especially in the World Championship Final.) I won that leg by a long way, but I couldn't stop Merv from winning the next and, with it, the first set. I had a shot at double 20 to win that leg but missed it. This wasn't a good sign either, because Merv hadn't missed any doubles yet and, as everyone knows, if you can't hit your doubles you're stuffed.

So there I was, one set down and, apart from a few decent throws, not doing very well at all. The first leg of the second set was tight, but I closed it out with a double 16 on my first try at a finish. After that, my arm started feeling a bit looser and my throw began to get smoother.

THE PEAK

After I won the third leg with a double 16 and made it one set all, I started to get a bit pumped up. When I saw the dart had landed in the perfect place, I didn't move after I followed through, just left my arm out there for a second or two and said to myself, *Here we go, now you're playing.*

I was on the way.

I won the first two legs of the third set, but made a right mess of things when I needed 32 to win the third leg and that set. I got a single 16 rather than a double, then a single eight rather than a double; when I needed a double four, I hit a single. It was terrible darts, really shitty play. Eric Bristow would not have been impressed.

After throwing like rubbish, I fully expected to lose the leg because Merv had 16 left. But whatever happened to me was obviously infectious, as he hit a single eight rather than the double he needed, got no score on his second dart and landed a single four with his last one, which left both of us on four. We were playing ridiculously badly. Normally, neither of us would let our game slip that far – we were professional players, not first-timers in a pub – but in a World Championship Final, when the tension mounts, funny things can happen.

Then I missed my first shot at double two. *Shit, this can't be happening*, I thought to myself. My dart had blocked most of the bed as well, so I had to move to the side to throw around it. Taking a deep breath, I launched it. Luckily, it landed where I wanted it to this time, so I was up two sets to one.

At this stage my three-dart average was 96, while Merv's was 88. It put me in a very strong position. I'd got some big throws in when I needed them, and I felt good.

A 180 with my first three darts at the start of the fourth

set gave me another boost, especially when Merv could only get 80 in reply. I finished that leg in 11 darts and I was on my way again. But Merv broke back and we got to two-all, with me throwing second in the decider. I started with 139, which put the pressure back on Merv, and took the leg.

A lead of three sets to one was a great position for me to be in at that stage. It made me stupidly relax a bit, at which point Merv came storming back and won the first two legs of the fourth set very quickly. They were over almost before they'd started and suddenly the momentum was with him, not me. I knuckled down and took the fourth leg, but it wasn't enough and it was three-two in sets.

After five sets the players get a break. In the papers the next week it would say that, during the break, one of the finalists went straight to the practice board and started throwing, while the other sat down on a chair in the corner of the players' bar with two brandies and a beer. No prizes for guessing which one was me.

I was really only topping up what I'd been putting away all day. That morning is a bit of a blur to me now, but my wife Jenny tells me I got up at about 8am, had a shower, a pot noodle for breakfast and then got straight on the drink. Before I'd even left the hotel room I'd had half a bottle of brandy and a few bottles of Holsten Pils.

Then I went downstairs to do a load of interviews with TV, radio and newspaper reporters. All the way through I had either a bottle of Pils or a brandy in my hand, or sometimes one of each. I drank solidly right up to the start of the match.

During the break, Jenny and our kids – Raymond and Emily – came to see me while I was backstage. Jenny and Emily had planned to watch the game from the back of the room, with the rest of the family, but couldn't see well enough; after the break they came right up to the stage and stood there, screaming and shouting, right up until the end.

When I watch the final on telly now, it's not my size I'm most embarrassed about. Although I can hardly believe it these days, and I hate the thought of what I must have looked like, I know the big lump up there on the stage is me. But what really make me cringe are that big lump's shoes.

For the entire tournament I wore these big white trainers – good quality Asics running shoes – with the tongues stuck right out in front of the bottom of my black trousers, as far as they could go. I thought I looked superb – when Emily told me how much she hated what I'd done with my trainers, I didn't listen to her!

This was the first time my dad, Syd, had come to watch me play for a long while. Normally I wouldn't let him come and see my big matches, because he'd put me off. He was a nightmare – always talking when everyone else was quiet. He didn't do it deliberately (he just likes talking), but he has a really loud voice which meant I could always hear him above everyone else, shouting, 'Come on Andrew!' No one else calls me Andrew, so I knew when he was around. This time he stayed at the back with my mum, Maureen.

After the break a different referee came out. It was George Noble, a top ref and also a very close mate of mine. George had asked if he could do the second half of the final, so he would be able to call 'game shot' for me if I won. He was another of the great friends who'd supported me so much; I wanted to win as much for them and my family as for myself.

When I walked back out onto the stage the noise was unbelievable. It almost knocked me backwards. I looked out into the crowd and there were Viking hats everywhere, plastic helmets with horns sticking out from the sides. So many people were cheering for me, and to hear them all was incredible. Jenny said later that she thought 95 per cent of the crowd were cheering for me, but I'm not sure that's right – I reckon my supporters were just louder and more pissed than Merv's!

In the first leg after the break, the beginning of the sixth set, my seventh dart was loose and landed in the five bed. I'd probably had one brandy too many.

With the scores that close, it wasn't what I needed. The pressure was on. Then I landed two big scores – a treble 20 and a treble 19 – to recover. I wasn't sharp and I'd lost that leg. I started the second badly too, with just 43, but, luckily for me, Merv could only come up with 38 in reply and I took the leg.

It was a key moment in the game. If Merv won the set, it would be three-all and if I won I'd be up four-two. We were playing best of 11 and the first to six sets would be World Champion, so a lead of two at this stage was actually huge.

Merv was fired up, the crowd were getting excited and I was just trying to stay calm. It got to two-all and Merv threw first in the decider. He set himself up well and had a shot at 64 for the leg. But he missed a double four to finish and had four left. I was on 104 but couldn't pull it out of the bag and left myself on 32, a straightforward double but one I might not even get a shot at because I'd given Merv a chance to win the leg before I had my next darts.

Merv missed his first shot at double four. I thought I might have a chance, but his second one went in and that was it – scores level at three sets each. Merv was coming back and I didn't like it. He'd handled the pressure better than me in that set, which wasn't a good sign. My average for those five

8

legs was 101 while his was only 93, and yet he'd managed to win the set. I needed to move up a gear or I was in trouble. I was outscoring Merv but not taking advantage because I was missing my doubles, the pressure shots, and he was hitting his.

I took the first leg of the seventh set comfortably and Merv took the second. In the third leg I had a wobble at the end, missing three doubles. But I struck lucky again because Merv got a bit careless in trying to close out from 101. He got his bull to leave 51 and then went for the single 19, which would have left him double 16 – a routine shot. But he was a bit casual and hit three – right next to the 19 – with his second dart instead.

That was a big moment. If he'd won that leg and punished me again for making mistakes on big throws, my head might have dropped. As it was, I landed my double 10 and the leg with my next dart. My confidence was up now, and it was Merv's head that you could see dropping a bit.

I won the next leg, and with it the set, but there was more work to do. Winning another set at four-three up would have meant I only needed one more set to win the match, but if I lost it we'd be even at four-all with everything still to play for.

At times like this darts becomes quite overwhelming. All these calculations about legs and sets and trebles and doubles are going through your mind at the same time as the crowd are making the most noise you've ever heard in your life. On top of this, you know your family are out there supporting you.

Oh, and there's a World Championship at stake too. No one ever said darts was an easy game!

I managed to keep my focus, scored heavily early in the

first leg of the eighth set and took it. All I had to do now was hold my own throws and I'd be five-three up. But Merv is a top player and wasn't going to make it easy for me. I missed a lot of doubles at the end of the second leg and Merv punished me by hitting his. That meant I didn't have the advantage of throwing first anymore, because Merv had won a leg on my throw. These legs were the most important of the match. Four-all or five-three – it all hinged on those darts.

We both missed doubles at the end of the third leg, but it was me who hit one first with my 16th dart. I'd been finishing legs with 11 or 12 earlier in the game, but that's how the pressure affects players as the match goes on.

I'd taken a leg against the darts and the pressure was now back on Merv to attack me on my throw. We were both on 261 after six darts, then 169 after nine. Neither of us wanted to give anything away.

With 161 left, I ideally wanted to score a couple of treble 20's but with my first two darts only managed singles, leaving me 121. Down around seven o'clock on the board is the 19 bed, with the treble – at 57 it's the second highest score available on the board – in the middle of it. Every darts player knows how important it is to be able to hit treble 19 when you need to. You might have blocked the treble 20 bed, or you might need an odd number to make your score up to an even one for the double to finish. In either case it's a crucial shot, and, on 121, a treble 19th would have left me a very achievable 64 to put the pressure right back on Merv.

It was a high-pressure throw, and I hit it.

But Merv came back and left himself with 70, so I knew he'd have a good chance of finishing if I didn't get the job done. I wanted treble 16 and then double eight, both straightforward shots. I got the treble with my first dart and thought, *Here we go, this is a big opening.*

But I missed my first go at the double eight. The crowd went quiet because they knew how important those darts were. And then I missed the second one too.

Now Merv had a chance. Under normal circumstances 70 is a comfortable finish, but these weren't normal circumstances as I'd shown when I missed my 64. Merv wasn't in the final by chance. He showed how good he is by nailing that 70 with two darts. Now I was in trouble because he was throwing first in the last leg of the set, and had a great opportunity to take us level again.

I'd blown my big chance. Would I get another one?

Neither of us did anything spectacular for the first few darts. We were neck and neck until Merv hit a good score to leave himself a straightforward finish of 80 while I still had a much trickier 139 to get. I had to finish the leg right there. It was all or nothing – we'd either be level at four-all or I'd be up five-three and a big favourite for the title.

I started with a treble 20, *bang* – right in the middle! Next was a treble 13. My dart crept in the corner of the bed, a couple of millimetres further and it would have missed. Finally, I needed a double 20, but I'd been missing loads of doubles and more double tops than any other all day. In fact, I hadn't landed a single one for the entire match. This one had to hit or the title would start slipping away from me.

I tried to clear my mind, took a deep breath and threw.

My dart flew perfectly, right into the middle of the board. But I couldn't celebrate, all I felt was relief.

John Part, who was commentating, described that dart as 'a heartbreaker for Mervyn King', and he was right. That was the moment the match went my way. I was five-three up and had finally started hitting the big shots. The crowd started chanting my name and I knew I had the upper hand. I was one set away from being World Champion.

But Merv wasn't finished (the stubborn sod!). Like all good players, he doesn't know when he's beaten. At the end of the next leg, after I'd thrown first, I missed yet another double 20 and he punished me again by going out on 110. He'd won a leg against my throw and I had to fight back, or we'd be in for a 10th set.

I didn't start well in the next leg. I was about 170 behind and Merv was trying to make a move. He had 45 left, I had two 218 and it was my throw. 134 kept me in touch, but Merv took it and I was two legs down. I had to fight back, and so I took the next two legs to make us even again. I would now throw first in the fifth and final leg of the ninth set – which could win me the world title. It was all in my hands. My dream was there for the taking.

I opened up with a 140 and Merv came back with 97. One more decent score and I'd be a long way ahead. I scored 100, which wasn't perfect but it was enough, because Merv came back with 40, leaving him on 364 and me on 261. And it was my turn to throw next.

Another hundred and I was comfortably ahead. Merv needed a big score but only hit 85, leaving him on 279. Yet another hundred put me on 61. Merv scored 60 next, which meant he was stuck on 219 and I had six darts to attain a score of 61 and become World Champion.

This was it – I was throwing for the match and the tournament. The World Championship. The big one. I'd reached four semi-finals before, but this was my first final. I'd beaten the world number one to get here and the biggest prize was there for the taking. Merv was a great player, but I knew I had him beaten. The trophy was mine to lose.

Andy Fordham, World Champion – I liked the sound of that. But I wasn't there yet. I still had to score 61. I knew I had six darts to finish the job, but I only wanted to use two. I knew this finish, I'd done it thousands of times before. Treble 15, double eight. Bang, bang. Job done. Easy.

But I'd never had to throw 61 to win the World Championship before. I let go the first dart – and it missed.

Instead of treble 15, it landed in the next bed, the treble 10. *Lucky.* 30 scored meant I still had to get another 31. It would be another straightforward finish with five darts in the bank, no problem. I'd have to use three darts after all. These were routine shots – a single 15 and a double eight.

The second dart landed straight in the middle of the 15 bed. That was better. Suddenly I could feel tears in my eyes, but fought them back. *Don't cry, you silly fat bastard,* I told myself, *you haven't won yet.*

Everyone who's ever played a darts match knows the last dart is always the hardest. It's the one that matters most, which makes the difference between winning and losing. If you can't land your last dart, you'll never win anything. And this was the most important final dart I'd ever throw.

The crowd were going mental. I'd never heard noise like it before. There were thousands of them all cheering for me. It didn't feel real and I needed to focus on that dart, needed to concentrate. I'd kept my cool and shown no emotion all the way through the match. No grimaces and no smiles, no playing to the crowd and no showboating. I'd controlled myself perfectly.

But inside I was falling apart. Every hour I'd spent learning to play, every practice dart, every ounce of effort and energy and emotion I'd devoted to this game was about to pay off.

I thought of Jenny, Raymond and Emily, watching from somewhere out in the crowd. Of all the times I was away from them, playing darts. Of the things I missed as my kids grew up. And of the things I wanted them to have in the future. I thought of how I could have lost Jenny, how I'd never been able to imagine a life without her even when she was seriously ill.

The tears were definitely coming now. I wanted to make them all proud.

One more good dart and they would be.

I only needed 16 – double eight, one of the easiest on the board, my favourite double. I'd hit more of these than I could count, thousands and thousands of them. But I'd never had to hit one to win a World Championship before.

I took a deep breath. I told myself I was back on the practice board in the pub, needing to shut out all the noise and the intense heat up there.

It didn't work. I couldn't forget that there were thousands of people in the audience watching me and millions more watching on TV.

I raised the dart and focused on that little patch of red on the left outside edge of the ring, just below nine o'clock on the board. As I watched it fly through the air towards the board, everything went quiet.

A split second later, my life would change forever.

When my dart landed perfectly in the double-eight bed, I felt all the nervous tension disappear. I turned round and looked at Merv. He congratulated me and told me not to start crying.

I cuddled him and said, 'It's too late,' because I'd already burst into tears.

THE PEAK

It was a great feeling, one of the best of my life. It's up there with my kids being born, one of unbridled joy and happiness. I might have forgotten a few things over the years, but I remember that moment as clearly as if it happened yesterday.

Merv got his runner-up trophy and then it was time for the magic words: 'Ladies and gentlemen, to receive a cheque for £50,000 and the championship trophy, the 2004 Lakeside World Professional Darts Champion . . . Andy Fordham!'

The noise of the crowd, the cheering and shouting, was fantastic. What a feeling!

I came down off the stage. Jenny and the kids were there, as were my nieces and nephews, my mum and dad and Jenny's dad. It was mad. When you win the title, everyone wants to grab you for an interview as soon as they can. I spoke to Ray Stubbs from the BBC first – a lovely bloke who became a good mate over the years. I was glad it was Ray I spoke to, because he was genuinely happy for me. I wasn't much of an interviewee, though. I was so emotional I could hardly talk.

At this stage, it hardly felt real. I found out a bit later that my average in the final was better than Merv's – 32.26 per dart compared to 30.34 – so I didn't fluke it. Seeing the numbers made me just about believe I'd done it. I also heard that one of the commentators, Tony Green, described my style that night as, 'rock solid at the oche and fluency within the arm'. Funny, I always thought I just stood there and threw it!

Jenny always says she can tell when I'm playing well because, if I'm on my game, I don't look around between darts. I just stand there, look down, rub my nose and pick up the next one. Apparently I was doing that from the start against Merv.

15

That's not my only funny habit when I play. When I win a leg, for some reason I lick my lips. (I don't mean to. I mean, it's not part of my game plan or anything.) Other players have them too: Daryl Fitton flexes his muscles when he wins and Tony O'Shea beats his chest. Daryl is a joker and sometimes he does all three – licks his lips, flexes his muscles and then beats his chest. I have no idea how he remembers to do all those things in the middle of a game!

I'm not superstitious, but I did wear the same shirt for every game except the first one. After it was on telly, I got a message from my mate Andy Jenkins saying, 'Change that shirt, you twat, it's too tight.' He was right – it was almost cutting off the circulation to my hands so I got another one. I then wore the same one every day for the rest of the tournament.

(Don't worry, it was clean every time. Tina, the step-daughter of Bob Potter, owner of the Lakeside Country Club which hosts the BDO World Championships, kindly took it home every night and washed it for me.)

A lot of people helped me out that week, but the one who did the most for me was Jenny. I've been so lucky with her. A lot of the other players' wives are on their case all the time to do this, that or the other for them, but Jenny has never done that. She just supported me and my darts playing. She'd make sure I was up in the morning, had everything I needed and then leave me alone to do what I had to do. I wouldn't have achieved anything if it wasn't for her. In fact, I honestly don't know what my life would have been like if I hadn't met Jenny.

She was as good as gold that week. Some of the wives get the hump when their husbands lose, which is something Jenny has never, ever done. She'd just shrug her shoulders and that would be it. It probably helps that she's not really interested in darts and doesn't understand it either. I remember telling her once that she should try to mix with the other wives a bit more. She came back afterwards and told me how she was listening to them talk about how their husbands had been playing and how high or low their averages were. Obviously they'd been watching their husbands' games very closely. But when they asked Jenny what my average was, she didn't have a clue. 'Oh, I don't know, about 24 bottles of beer a day,' she said. They didn't really involve her in their conversations after that.

Jenny says that if I was a plasterer or a plumber she wouldn't come and watch me working, so why would she watch me playing darts? She didn't miss the final, though, and I think she enjoyed the game too.

I went on to the Champions' Reception afterwards and had to make a speech, but I don't remember any of it. (I'd like to see a tape of it, if one exists.) Normally people get up there and thank everyone – the BDO, the BBC, their family, friends, dog, and so on. Knowing how my mind works, I probably got up there and said something like, 'I'm not going to stand here thanking everyone, because we all know what they do to make this happen and we all appreciate it. Have a great night. Now, can I please have a drink?'

The only thing I remember is making sure that I didn't go in until Trina Gulliver, the Women's World Champion, arrived, so we could walk in together. I know Tina would have waited for me so I did the same for her.

A strange thing happened about two months later, when I was in Spain for a series of exhibitions called Fun in the Sun. This girl came up with a picture of her and me with the trophy from that night. I was so pissed you couldn't even see my eyes. She said the photo was taken at about 1:30am that night, but I don't remember it. (Then again, I don't remember much from that period, so it's hardly surprising.)

Jenny said I seemed overwhelmed by the fact that I'd become World Champion. I'd only ever been a semi-finalist before and the level of interest in me was a huge shock. It made me anxious, so I drank even more to cope with it. I was up until about 2am that night, when I finally ran out of steam.

The next day, Robert Holmes, press man for the BDO, took me to do another interview for local TV. After that, we set off home to the pub that we own. Steve Walsh, a friend who helped me out during the tournament, drove, and it took us about 45 minutes to get back. I was so knackered by the time we left that all I wanted to do was have a few drinks with the regulars – the people who I saw day in, day out – and then go to bed. Finally I could relax.

But when we pulled up at The Rose we couldn't even get through the front door, because there were TV crews, radio, local and national papers all waiting for me – as well as all the locals, friends and family. It was absolute bedlam. The staff had decorated the pub with balloons and bunting, there were so many cameras flashing and questions flying at me that it felt unreal – great, but unreal. I finally got to bed at about 10:30pm, absolutely shattered.

The next day was the same. The pub phone was ringing off the hook, as was the phone upstairs, my mobile and Jenny's mobile. I basically handed my phone to Jenny and said, 'Here, you handle it.' There were so many calls that she had to get her friend to help her with answering them all, taking down numbers and messages. A lady from the *Daily*

18

Mail came to see me but I was so tired I refused to get out of bed. She wanted to talk to me up in our room, but Jenny said, 'No way,' – or probably something much less polite – because she had to draw the line somewhere. (I said that if the woman came back the next day I'd see her, but not to come too early. In fact she ended up writing a very nice article about me.)

Now that I was World Champion, everyone was interested in me. There was either a camera crew, a radio presenter or a newspaper reporter waiting for me in the pub every day for at least two weeks. I also had commitments for live darts exhibitions and was being pulled from pillar to post. Jenny said I was a bit overwhelmed by it all, and seemed to need a drink before seeing or talking to anyone. It was my way of coping.

Not long after that, Dave, my manager at the time, got me a place on *Celebrity Fit Club*, the reality TV show. I didn't want to go on, so Jenny and Dave tried everything they could think of to make me sign the contract because they could see I needed help. I was getting bigger and bigger and my health was deteriorating, but I would not listen.

I wish I had.

TWO

EARLY DAYS

I threw my first competitive darts in a pub in Greenwich called the Angerstein Hotel, when I was 19 years old. It was just up the road from where I grew up in Charlton, southeast London, in the house where my parents still live now. We'd moved there from another, smaller place close by, on Christmas Eve 1964, when I was nearly three. There was a little drama that took place there almost straight away.

It was freezing cold on the day we moved in, and my mum wanted to give me a drink of warm Ribena because she was worried about the weather getting to me. The bloke who lived there before us worked for the gas board, so there were gas mantles all over the house because he used them much more than the electricity. There was a heater directly over the sink which did the hot water and there were three taps under it, but there was electricity as well so it was all a bit confusing.

When she needed some warm water for my Ribena, my mum took it out of the first tap she tried which wasn't cold.

What she didn't know at the time was that the tap went up to the square tank in the roof – the one powered by electricity, not gas. It hadn't been used in 30 years, but it still had water in it. You can imagine the state of what came out.

The water had become so poisonous over the years that it actually turned red, but because it mixed with Ribena as soon as it came out my mum didn't notice. That stuff must have been nearly radioactive. Over the next few days I started feeling more and more weird. I couldn't walk without losing my balance; I couldn't talk properly; I was hot, and sick, and really out of sorts. I got a little tricycle for Christmas and couldn't even ride it. I was so ill that the doctor was seriously worried about me, and my parents were absolutely terrified.

Luckily, the doctor looked after me brilliantly. After a few days he gave me penicillin and I gradually got better. They still didn't know exactly what it was, but they thought it was typhoid or something similar.

Eventually, they realised what had happened when someone turned on the tap and red water came out. After that, my dad went up and checked the pipes. They were so clogged up that you couldn't even get a knitting needle through them; I'm not surprised that I was so ill!

(I wouldn't really understand how scared they would have been until I had my own children, years later. When my boy, Raymond, stayed out all night once, I was in a right state. You don't really understand those feelings until you have kids of your own. And, if you're anything like me, that's when *you* start feeling guilty about what you put your own parents through.)

The people who sold the house to us were originally supposed to move out in the July of that year. My dad had been to see it in the spring and loved the garden, because it was far bigger than the one we had before. The old one had enough space for a shed outside, and that was it. My dad said walking into the new one felt like stepping into Epping Forest because it was so big. So they decided to go for it, because I was starting to run around and my parents had already had more kids.

Then they found out that the bloke was staying for another six months after my dad made his offer, but the guy said he wouldn't sell it to anyone else, even if they offered a lot more than my parents had. It was unbelievably nice of him. As if that wasn't enough, he said he'd pay half the interest on the bridging loan my parents had to get to buy the house. There was no reason at all for him to be so kind, so we were really lucky. That house was perfect for us, and Mum and Dad have been in it for almost 50 years now.

It was in 1963, the year after I was born, that my parents had the twins, John and Julie; they'd be followed, in 1968, by my sister Tracy. After that, my parents stopped. Four kids were enough for them.

We didn't have a lot of money, but my dad worked hard and we had everything we needed and more. Like holidays. We used to go to these camps in Spain and France every year, and they were a really good laugh. My dad is very loud and he'll talk to anyone, so we always made friends with people.

It also gave me my first taste of the downside of drinking alcohol.

It happened in Spain when I was about 15, before I was old enough to really know what a hangover was. I had a few drinks one night and then the next day I went down to the beach on my own. I lay face down on the sand for a rest and went straight to sleep. I hadn't told anyone where I was going, and so when they realised I wasn't around my family started panicking.

Eventually they found me, and I was like a lobster. I'd been asleep on my front in the sunshine for hours and my skin was in agony. When I lay in bed that night I could see a huge spider crawling all over me; I absolutely hate spiders, but I was in so much pain I couldn't even move to get it off me.

Another summer, we went to Italy with my mate Colin and his parents. My dad gave me some foreign money for the first time, something like 10 million lira, and I thought I was the richest boy in the whole place. I couldn't believe how much money I had – 10 million, imagine that! Before I decided what to spend my new riches on, I needed a can of Coke and a bag of crisps to help me think; once I'd paid for them, I only had about half a million lira left. I didn't get quite so excited about Italian money after that.

I did okay at school – not brilliantly, but okay. But I bawled my eyes out on my first day at the Cherry Orchard Primary School. My mum took me and I didn't want to go in. A bit later in the day, my mum and my nan walked round and saw me standing on my own in the playground, not talking to anyone and looking miserable. It must have been difficult for them, but after that I was fine. Once I'd settled in and made friends, I liked it so much that I'd turn up early so I could play football.

As I got older, I began to get distracted quite easily from the more serious things in life. I was more interested in going out and having fun with my mates. When I was 16 or 17 I used to go out and not tell my parents where I went. I wouldn't get back till four in the morning. It happened a few times, and eventually my dad said he'd had enough. If I wasn't in by ten o'clock he'd lock the door. The next time it happened, that's exactly what he did. (I had to bang on the door until he let me in.)

At the time, I had an apprenticeship as a plumber with a good company, and it drove my dad up the wall to think I was wasting it by staying out to all hours with my mates. To be fair, he was right, because I didn't finish it. I had to go to one evening class a week and in the end, because I was hardly going to it, my dad used to drive me down there. I'd walk in the front door, hide and watch him until he drove away and then run out and get the bus back to the pub, where all the lads were.

When I was on the apprenticeship course there was a bloke working there called Brian Glenister, who was one of the funniest blokes I ever met. He was always naked – always. At work he'd just strip off for no reason. The first time I met him he grabbed me by the nuts. I asked him what he was doing but he told me not to worry because he was only being friendly. Unbelievable! And he just wouldn't wear pants, ever. We'd walk in to get changed before the course, and the first time we were in there he just stripped off with nothing underneath. I thought, 'What the hell's going on here?' I'd heard of initiations before but I hadn't expected anything like this.

They asked my dad to make me carry on the apprenticeship, but my mates said I could earn more as a labourer so I packed it in. My dad was right in the end. After I left the apprenticeship there wasn't even a job for me as a labourer.

My dad was a plumber and an electrician, and he rightly wanted me to have the same stable life that he did. My problem was that I didn't like working, I much preferred having a laugh. I know that sometimes I didn't make life easy for my parents, but I never got into drugs or anything like that so I wasn't *that* bad.

I had a hobby when I was younger which always surprises people. I was really into birds. (The ones with feathers, I mean.) I wanted an aviary in the garden and was a member of the YOC, the Young Ornithologists' Club. I used to love to go out birdwatching in the garden and in the woods, nowhere really far away. I used to love drawing them too, it was a very peaceful pastime. When I was about 16 I had a couple of yellow budgies which I kept in my room. I used to let them fly around and then I'd have to catch them by throwing a jumper over them one at a time. My room wasn't big but it wasn't easy to do, because they were nippy little things. (Once I took them up to my cousin in Scotland, and sat with their cage on my lap for the whole journey.)

As I got a little bit older I started playing football on Sundays. They called me 'the Whippet' because I was fast. People think I made that up, but it's true. It didn't last long, though. As I put on a bit of weight my speed started to go. Eventually I moved into midfield and became one of those really competitive, energetic players. I used to get sent off quite a lot, usually for bad tackles when I got carried away, except for once when I swore at the referee and got banned. That was a stupid thing to do, even though he'd just made a terrible decision.

I've always been into football and have supported Glasgow Rangers since I was a kid. It's not an obvious team for a lad from southeast London to follow, but we have family living up in Scotland. My Uncle Mick, who has sadly passed away now, was a Rangers fan. He and some of his mates used to come down to stay with us in Charlton every other year for the England vs. Scotland game, before all the problems with hooligans and violence meant they had to be cancelled.

My aunt used to phone up my mum and dad and tell them there would be four blokes coming down for the game, but by the time they arrived there would be at least 12 of them. The extras were usually people they'd met on the train who needed somewhere to sleep. But my parents didn't mind at all because we used to have such a laugh with them. They'd put the Rangers songs on and we'd all be singing and dancing around to them in the front room. Then, at about eight o'clock in the morning, they'd be having their breakfast with a can of Tartan lager. After that we'd all be outside, playing football before they went off to the match; we were really young then, and they used to give me and my brother and sisters a fiver to clean their shoes. We loved it.

Everyone in the area knew when they were here. One year the piper came, a pal of my uncle who played the bagpipes. He started playing in the morning and my mum and dad thought it was just a matter of time before the neighbours started complaining. Sure enough, a few minutes after he started there was a knock on the door. But it wasn't a complaint. The neighbours said they couldn't hear him playing as well as they wanted, so would he mind going out into the road to play for everyone? He also played at our local pub, The Swan, and they loved him there too. The same guy ended up on the front page of the *Daily Mirror*, playing the bagpipes and leading the Scotland fans up Wembley Way for the game.

I was about 12 when I went to see my first Rangers game with my uncle, an away game against Hibs. After the match we all ended up on the pitch and it was mayhem – there were people screaming, fighting, all sorts. At that age I thought it was an amazing adventure. We used to go up to Scotland a lot, several times a year from when I was two up to about the age of 15, because my nan and my mum's sister moved up there. I remember walking up to Arthur's Seat in Edinburgh, near Murrayfield rugby ground a few times; they were great holidays.

Over the years – once I started doing well at the darts and getting more well-known – when people found out I was a Rangers fan I started getting invited to their do's, where I'd meet people who'd invite me to the games. That's how I became friends with Andy Goram, who's now one of my very best mates. I've had too many great nights up there to mention with Andy – or 'the Goalie', as he's known. After I won the World Championship I was supposed to take the trophy up to Rangers and show it off to the fans before a game, but I had a bad back so I couldn't go. I was gutted about that. I'd have loved to walk out onto the pitch at Ibrox with my trophy, it would have been a dream come true.

I haven't been up for a few years now and I miss it. The glory years – watching the team which won nine championships in a row with players like Hateley and McCoist – were so great, but I'm sure I'll get back up there one day.

Rangers aside, George Best was my football idol when I was younger. He was a great player, of course, but I also liked his long hair. I played on the wing too, but I didn't grow my hair long because of him though. My dad didn't want me to, which made me keen to do it. (My mum didn't mind it that much, as long as it looked clean and shiny.)

I had always wanted a beard and moustache, and grew them as soon as I could – which meant I had them when I left school. In fact, I have only ever shaved once in my entire life. It was on my 18th birthday and I was as pissed as a fart, so I wasn't exactly gentle with the razor. When I finished I'd cut my face to ribbons and blood was pouring down my face. My brother – smartarse that he was – gave me some aftershave to put on. He poured loads on my hands and told me to splash it on my face because it would make the cuts better. I didn't know how much I was supposed to use, so I threw the stuff all over my face really quickly. Then I was in agony. I sobered up quite quickly after that. (Quickly enough to chase my brother round the house, anyway.)

Jenny has been with me for 30 years and has only ever seen me without a beard twice – the first time on my 18th birthday. We'd started going out the year before, when I was 17 and she was 15. We met in a pub called the Bugle Horn in Charlton Village. I was sitting at the bar and I saw this long hair and a really, *really* nice arse. And that was that.

I was quite shy in those days, so the best I could do for a chat-up line was offer her a lift home. She said okay, thinking I was older than I was and would have my own car or bike. All I had was my mate with his car outside, but she didn't seem to mind and got in anyway.

Then, when we got to her house, she'd forgotten her key. The next thing I knew, she was climbing up the front of the house to her window like something out of the SAS. She finally got in and came down to open the door. By then I was a bit scared (I told you I was shy!), so I went home. But we carried on from there, we lived close to each other and I saw her out a lot. It's amazing, really, that we've spent more than 30 years together and I'm as happy with her now as I've ever been. Maybe it's because of everything we've been through.

The second time Jenny saw me without a beard came when I had a makeover for a newspaper recently. They trimmed it really short to what they called a 'shadow', and she wasn't happy with that. It was the first time in 25 or 30 years that a proper hairdresser had touched my hair, because I've been cutting it myself for all that time. I have my own system: I brush it forward, cut the front, cut the sides and brush it back into place.

The hair at the back hadn't been touched at all since I was last in a hairdresser's, and I must admit it was getting a bit straggly. When I was young and out working with my dad, which I did every now and then in those days, he always used to have a go at me about my hair. It made me more determined to keep it long. One day, when I was about 19, we were doing some work in a hairdresser's and he asked if I wanted to get it cut there. He knew I was lazy and, seeing as we were in the right place already, it wasn't like I'd have to go far to have it done. I told him to piss off, and he said he was only joking. If I wanted to have long hair, that was fine by him.

After that, my attitude changed a bit. Now that it didn't annoy my dad anymore, maybe I'd get it cut. So I asked one of the girls in the shop if she'd do it; I remember her grabbing my ponytail with one hand, picking up some scissors with the other and cutting off a huge lump of hair. I was fine with it and went home happy, but Jenny was furious. That's probably why I didn't get it cut properly for another 25 years. (I use hairspray now, extra firm Silvikrin. I'll get stick for admitting it but I don't care.)

The long hair was all part of the image in the early 1970s, when my favourite band was T.Rex. I liked them and my brother liked Slade, then I liked Status Quo, who are good in concert. I got really into my heavy rock after that, which may be part of the reason why I had long hair. You could say I was a biker without a bike. I listened to Led Zeppelin and things like that, and I remember going to Hammersmith to see AC/DC one night and Motorhead the next.

Those were brilliant days, and I used to spend quite a lot of time rollerskating as well. We'd do it in Greenwich and, believe it or not, I was actually quite good. I really enjoyed it, too, until I was pushed over and knocked out one of my front teeth.

I have a few tattoos from back then. The one on my right arm says 'Bof' at the top, because that was my nickname when I was younger. It's short for Boffin, which was a joke as I wasn't the sharpest tool in the box at school. The picture below it is a skull with hair and underneath it the words say, 'Beauty is only skin deep.' It's a bit faded and if I could change it I would. But it's too late now. On my left arm there's the Grim Reaper, and I don't want to get rid of that one.

I've got one on my hand which is supposed to be a shooting star, but it looks more like a star that's been shot and is falling out of the sky. It was supposed to be shooting out of the skin between my finger and thumb, but didn't work out that way. (It's a bit of a mess, actually.)

I've also got one on my back, which is supposed to be a swallow with Jenny's name under it. I had it done in Blackpool when I went there for a weekend. I bought Jenny a big teddy bear and when I got back I told her I had two big surprises for her. First there was the bear, and then I took my shirt off and showed her the tattoo. I was expecting her to be touched by it, and to think I'd been really sweet. But she didn't react like that at all.

'That doesn't look like my name. It looks like "Jerry", the cartoon mouse,' she said. 'Why have you got it on your back? Are you ashamed of it?' It wasn't quite what I was hoping for.

There's another one on my leg which is supposed to be a

dog being sick, done by a Hells Angel with Indian ink. A few of my mates were in a band called the Tripe Hounds and that was going to be their logo. But the name changed and they got rid of it. What a total waste of time!

I was about 17 or 18 when I had the tattoos done on my arm; those on my leg and hand came a bit later, and then the one on my back was done in the 1990s, when I was playing darts. I don't really regret any of them, they're part of who I am now. But my parents never liked them.

I don't know what I'd think if my kids got tattoos. Emily can't have them because she has a bad heart and Raymond doesn't have any yet. I hope that, if he ever does get one, he thinks it through because it'll be with him forever.

These days my taste in music has mellowed, and I'm now more into Frank Sinatra, Dean Martin and Nat King Cole. In fact, 'Little Ole Wine Drinker Me' by Dean Martin should probably be my walk-on song. I still like a bit of rock though, and have actually started going to concerts again now I'm a bit healthier.

I'm a shit singer, mind you. I used to do a bit of karaoke back when I was drinking. 'Fly Me to the Moon' was my song, but my karaoke days ended when my drinking days ended. I might be able to play darts in front of a crowd without alcohol one day, but singing is a very different matter. Jenny and I did a song together at a charity do about 20 years ago, when we lived in Woolwich, we sang Sonny and Cher's 'I Got You Babe'. It was fun, but we were terrible.

Now we live in Thamesmead and run a pub called The Cutty Sark. Jenny and I have always lived in the same area of southeast London. The furthest we've been out is Dartford, Kent, which isn't very far at all. Before I was ill, we were going to get a pub down in Horsham, Sussex, but it fell through because I went to hospital. Now there's nowhere else I'd like to live in England. Maybe there'll be Scotland one day, but all our friends and family are around us here.

My history is all around the same area. It's where I grew up, met Jenny and first played darts. I started when I was 19, after Jenny introduced me to her uncle John at our engagement party in 1980. He played for the Angerstein Hotel's football team, and one day he asked me to go along and start training with them. I thought it might be fun, so I did. They were a great bunch, we had a right laugh and I started going regularly. I liked the atmosphere and being with the boys. We used to train on a Wednesday night and after that a few of the lads used to go and have a few drinks and play darts in the pub, so I went along too. One night they were short of a player for a match and asked me to play. I said, 'No way,' because at that point I'd never thrown a dart competitively, I'd only ever practised. But they said it was just a bit of fun so I did.

We were playing down in Greenwich at The Spanish Galleon. I was crap – I mean *terrible* – but I really, really enjoyed it. There was such a buzz around it. Some people have those moments in their lives when they do something for the first time and find they just want to do it as much as they possibly can. This was mine.

I already loved darts because of the great bunch of lads on the team. When that extra bit of competition was added I was hooked. I had such a laugh playing on the same team as those lads that I very quickly wanted more and more. If I'd gone onto a team full of boring old blokes it might not have had the same effect. But as it was, I couldn't get enough.

Once I started playing more, darts was no longer only for

fun. I wanted to get better and better. When I started playing, I'd see people going out on certain shots, big finishes, and I'd wonder how the hell they knew how to do it. Then I started picking up how the numbers worked, how different combinations of trebles and doubles fitted together and how to calculate what was the best shot to go for next.

The best way to learn was chalking, logging the scoring while other people were playing. You start adding up and taking away and it helps you understand how the numbers work from 501 down. In our league, everyone took turns chalking. If you lost, you chalked; after a while you learned how to do it and then you didn't want to chalk anymore. But once I'd learned to chalk I understood the game better, and my own game started improving.

From the very first time I played, every time I walked into a pub my darts were out before I'd even been to the bar. I wanted to play all the time. People got the hump with me, because I used to try to get them to play so much. It went on for about a year and I still wasn't very good, but then a guy called Stevie Lock and me won a pairs tournament for the Angerstein in the Greenwich Seven to Ten League. I went on to win the singles tournament as well, and a couple more in a row after that.

A few years after that a mate of mine took me to another pub, The Guildford Arms. It was run by a bloke called Kenny Tar and there were some good old players down there, proper players who were much better than any I'd seen before. Kenny got me playing in the Kent Super League and, after a while, put my name forward for the Kent County side. In between, I joined another team which played on another night of the week.

I wasn't really working much at the time. My plumbing

apprenticeship had lasted about a year and a half, and after that I became a bit of a rebel. After that I worked with my dad a fair bit on electrical stuff and plumbing. Then I worked at Makro's, the cash and carry place. It was a huge warehouse and I was out the back at Goods Receiving, I used to ticket them up as they came in. I didn't really mind the work but the money wasn't great. Even then, I was drinking. At lunch you'd get half an hour off, and I'd be out across the road and into the pub as quickly as I could for a couple of pints. (Okay, possibly three.) And some days I just wouldn't come back, which began to get me in a bit of shit after a while. I was about 23 or 24 then. When I stopped there I worked for a guy called Charlie Mills for a few years, we used to do heater casings. That was good money, but I never really stuck at anything apart from darts.

I started earning money from darts after I played my first World Championship – or Embassy Championship, as it was back then, in 1995 at the Lakeside. I'd been really lucky with Jenny, who was so very understanding about me concentrating on darts. We weren't that well off, Jenny worked in pubs and did a few other jobs to keep money coming in, but my main focus was darts and she supported that. After 1995 I'd start doing a few exhibitions and making money from those.

I never knew I was going to turn pro. I just enjoyed darts as a sport and treated it as a hobby more than anything else. I only played for fun but I still wanted to get better. I'd always been a sporty person and I suppose that made me competitive – I wanted to improve. Still, I never thought about making a living from darts. I just loved playing and getting better.

You get selected for the county team if your three-dart

average in the Super League is good enough. You have two teams, the A team and the B team, and then the reserves. People were telling me I should be picked, so I started putting myself up for it. For about three months, when the team was announced I'd be looking for my name in the reserves. I wasn't picked. I didn't like the tension, so I thought I'd look the next month and, if I didn't make it, I'd take myself out of the running. But then the letter came through. I looked at the reserves and didn't see my name, so I just thought, *Bollocks, that's it then*. Then I looked at the B team and saw my name.

I only played about eight games for the B before I got picked for the A team, against Buckinghamshire. That was it. I was an A player from then on. It was brilliant fun, we all met up once a month and travelled around with our expenses paid.

We had Billy Dunbar, who was a great player, Peter Stanlick, a very good friend of mine, Nicky Norris, who's still playing now, Clarrie Farrell, another great character, Ian Carpenter and then Ian Covil – who was one of the best, most natural darts players I've ever seen. If he'd had the same dedication as me he'd have been World Champion easily. But he'd get bored of it so quickly that he wouldn't bother. If he was in a competition he just wouldn't turn up; he'd rather be off fishing, which he was good at too.

There was a fun tournament called the Cockney Classic at the time, where the winner got to play Eric Bristow. They did an interview beforehand and said to Ian, 'Now you're going to play Bristow, are you excited about the money or the title?' He said, 'Neither, I just want to beat Bristow.' And he did.

Ian looked like a punk rocker, with white hair on one side and black on the other. He was another very funny man and would have gone down brilliantly in professional darts. He looked so unusual and was such a character that the crowds would have loved him.

When I had some success in local tournaments, my parents started to take an interest in my darts and came to watch me. At first I didn't mind at all, but it didn't take long for me to realise it wasn't always a good idea to have them there – or my dad, anyway.

I went to a place called Tenterton to play in a tournament of Working Men's Clubs from all over the country. I was playing for Kent when my mum and dad came down to watch with Jenny. We were underway and playing, two legs in, and it was my throw. I threw one dart and was about to throw my second when there was a tap on my shoulder. I turned round and my dad was standing there with a pint.

'What are you doing?' I said.

'You wanted a drink.'

'I know I did, but how about putting it on the table?'

'Well, I don't know what you want to do with it!'

That's my old man all over. I'm in the middle of throwing in a really important game and he comes up to give me a pint. Unbelievable! This was the first of many moments like that. I was playing in another tournament at Camber Sands once and there were about 800 people there watching. The atmosphere was loud and there was lots of banter flying around – I used to get called all kinds of things, 'fat boy', 'grizzly', all sorts, and I didn't mind.

But then I heard my dad pipe up: 'Come on, Andrew!' No one else calls me *Andrew* and it drives me crazy.

It got to the stage where I wouldn't let him come to the

World Championships because he was bound to do something embarrassing. But then, in 2004, my mum asked if he could come to watch me play the final. I said that of course he could, there was no way I'd let him miss the biggest game of my life – but it might be easier if he was in the backroom, watching it on TV. 'Fine,' said my mum. But, unbeknownst to me, they actually got him into the main auditorium with everyone else. There were about five people around him, and if ever he went to stand up and say something they just grabbed him and sat him down again. But I'd have been gutted if he'd missed it.

He doesn't mean to do it, he just says the wrong thing at the wrong times. After he gave me that drink at a CIU [Working Men's Club and Institute Union] game they asked him to be quiet and he said, 'I didn't say anything,' which just wound them up even more. Then, when he finally did stop talking, he'd start fiddling with the keys in his pocket. It's not deliberate, he just can't help it.

One of the highlights of my darts career came when I was picked to play for England for the first time. The person I have to thank more than any other for this is a man called Roger Nixon, who was one of the most important people in the early part of my darts career. He used to run a pub called The Morning Star and he had The Sydney Arms down in Lewisham.

I went down there and started playing for his pub; when he saw I had some talent, he took an interest in what I was doing. Roger was the one who convinced me to play for London rather than Kent in the county system, because the London team had a much higher profile and would help me get noticed by the England team, which in turn would help me get into the professional game.

In the early days he made me captain of his team and always pushed me to play at a higher level. Roger was brilliant like that. Being a publican to him was about much more than serving drinks. There was a real community there and Roger was at the centre of it. He knew everyone and looked out for them. He was the best publican I've ever known.

When I was playing for Roger's team I used to get Man of the Match awards quite regularly. The first time it happened, we won our match and then the food came out afterwards. I went to get some but they put it all miles away from me. I asked for some but Roger wouldn't let me have any food. I was hungry and not very happy about it. I couldn't understand why I wasn't allowed any.

Unbeknownst to me, Colleen Noble, the wife of George Noble Senior (my mate George's dad, who sadly passed away a short while ago, after a long illness), had been cooking this special pie all day. She called it a Desperate Dan cow pie, an enormous thing with two horns sticking out. So I was sitting there, hungry and confused about why Roger wouldn't let me have any food, when this massive pie appeared as my special treat for winning Man of the Match. The thing was delicious, but it was so big that I could only eat about a quarter of it. I wrapped up the rest and took it home.

Roger is in a class of his own. He's a great character who's been around for years and everyone respects him because of everything he's done for the game. He's had some great teams and organised the tournament sponsored by the *News Shopper*, our local paper, which was a big deal in darts.

We used to sit down and have a few chats about my darts. Roger was really supportive and wanted me to progress in the game. He actually ended up putting me forward to play for Scotland. The way it worked was that when you started playing for a county – I was playing for London by then – you put your averages forward to the team representing the part of the UK you wanted to play for. The England team was really strong and there wasn't much chance of me getting in there, so we tried to put me forward for Scotland because my granddad was Scottish.

The other big motivation was the extra ranking points you got for playing internationals. Those points would help you get into the Embassy World Championship, which was the ultimate goal for every player, the door to the professional stage. But a guy called John Cook knocked me back from the Scotland team because I'd lost a few games. It would be a year or so before my averages went forward to England and I got in. I've never looked back.

I think of myself as British – I was born and brought up in England and support the England football team, but I have Scottish family and support Rangers too. But if I could choose a country to play for, it would be England every time. When I actually got picked, I couldn't believe it. I had no idea it was coming. I was playing in a competition at a mate's pub called The Rising Sun, up on the Old Kent Road, when someone told me there was a phone call for me. It was a bloke called Sam Hawkins, who was one of the selectors. I got called over the phone and he said, 'Hi Andy, I just wanted to let you know you've been picked for England.'

I was absolutely gobsmacked. There isn't much more you can wish for than representing your country, and to this day it is up there with the World Championship as one of my proudest achievements. I did it for a few years in the end, playing for England in many different countries and at World Cups, and I loved it. I was so proud to be playing for my country, and I remain proud to this day.

There were a few professional players involved, but I wasn't one of them at the start. I didn't get paid for it but it didn't matter, they just covered my expenses. The first time I played for back to England was at the Lakeside. It was a two-day tournament between us, Wales and Scotland. I played both days and won the first one against Wales, but lost the second against Scotland.

I've still got a shirt signed by all the England players in the team that day. There was Steve Beaton, Martin Adams and Trina Gulliver, who was Ladies' World Champion for about seven years on the trot and is a legend of the women's game. It was her first tournament too. My dad had come along and was really, really proud – as well as a bit overexcited, as usual. Trina came over in her full England outfit – white shirt and bright red trousers, very smart – and wanted a couple of items signed for her nephews. She asked me to sign them and my old man went, 'Oh look, it's another fan!'

I looked at him, then I looked at her, then I looked back at him and said, 'Dad, she plays for the team.' He's a funny one, my Dad. You have to meet him to believe him.

That was a great day. A load of friends came over to watch and stayed in the hotel. I got a bottle of champagne that night and we celebrated properly. I had never even dreamt of playing for England. I hadn't even expected to play county darts, let alone for my country. I did it all for fun. I'm a happy-go-lucky person and that was a happy-go-lucky time. I was never particularly ambitious, I just liked what I was doing.

The thing I enjoyed most about darts in the end was the friends you made. You'd all meet up more or less once a month and travel together abroad somewhere to play. We became like one big family and I loved that. There'd be some from London, some from up north and so on and you'd all meet up in Holland, Sweden, Germany or wherever, all together playing and drinking and having a great time. There was almost never any trouble at darts tournaments. Pubs close for some football matches because fans get pissed and start fights. But if you go to a darts match it doesn't happen, even though people are drinking properly all day – and when I say all day, I mean *all* day, from about eight in the morning to ten at night. Yet, throughout all the years I've been playing, you could count the number of times I've seen trouble on the fingers of one hand, with fingers left over too.

It's the competition, the atmosphere, the people, the fun. I got a taste for it all and it excited me. It made me work harder at it and that's why I got good at it.

Still, all the darts and drinking would begin to affect my health in the mid-90's. Looking back, I can see I buried my head in the sand and ignored it. I used to tell myself I was okay really because I didn't eat much. I've never been a big eater, actually. I used to eat fry-ups but they were never massive, just normal-sized ones – a couple of bits of bacon, a couple of sausages, an egg, black pudding if it was available. They weren't huge meals, but they didn't mix well with all the booze. I know that now.

Over the years I stopped doing any exercise as well. I used to play loads and loads of football and run everywhere. Even after I started drinking, when I was about 19 or 20 and put on a bit of weight, I was still really fit so I didn't mind. My mates called me Fatty Arbuckle but it didn't bother me.

Then I got a bad back and stopped doing all the healthy stuff like running and football, but carried on with the bad things. The competitive side of me which loved a game of football focused on darts instead. It's what made me so good in the end, but as I was playing more so I was drinking more. The result was that I got bigger.

When you put on weight gradually you don't realise it's building up, and neither do the people who live with you. When you're with someone all the time it's a fact that you don't notice small changes. When a man loses his hair, if you're not close to the bloke you might only see him once every two years; by then his fringe might start halfway back over his head, but his wife won't have noticed because she lives with him and sees him every day. It's the same with putting on weight. If someone hadn't seen me for a couple of years they'd have noticed, without question.

The old phrase about it being easy to put on weight but hard to get it off is also true, believe me. As it got worse I started doing less and less exercise. Eventually I would try to walk as little as possible. Once, when my clothes started getting too tight, I even blamed Jenny for shrinking my shirts.

THREE

ON THE ROAD

As I became a better player and moved up the ranking system, I started getting asked to play in bigger tournaments. This meant travelling to play abroad, which made me love darts even more. At the time I thought nothing could be better than going away with my mates for a few days to get on the beer and play darts.

The first big trip I had was to America in 1994. A guy called Jim Granahan sponsored me, which meant he paid for my travel in return for a share of my winnings. The tournament was intended to be a stepping stone to the Embassy, because I would get ranking points if I did well. Without Jim's investment I wouldn't have been able to afford to go. Sadly, he's dead now, but I'll always be grateful to him for his help.

I was looking forward to the darts, but leaving my family behind was horrible. Going to the airport and saying goodbye to Jenny and the kids was one of the hardest things I'd ever done. (I still have the napkins I picked up and wrote notes to

Raymond and Emily on.) Until then the longest I'd been away from them all was a weekend, but now I was going for two weeks. As I walked away from them into departures I couldn't bring myself to even turn around. I had tears in my eyes and I was a mess. If I'd had to look at them as well I'd have been even worse, and might not have gone at all. So I just marched through without looking over my shoulder.

I've always been a nervous flyer and this journey to Los Angeles was the longest flight I'd ever been on. I was shitting myself, if you'll pardon my French. I was lucky to get a seat with legroom near the front, but all the other lads on the flight were up at the back so I didn't think it'd be much fun for me on my own. I was right. When I sat down the bloke next to me was all suited up and looked very serious, while I was wearing tracksuit bottoms and putting away beers as fast as I could.

As it turned out, the only two words he said to me on the whole flight were, 'Excuse me,' when he wanted to go to the toilet. That didn't help my nerves at all, although I was well looked after by American Airlines. They'd bring beers up whenever you wanted and ask if you wanted a drink with your food, which meant plenty of cans of beer for me.

That trip was the first time I met a darts player called Tom Kirby. When I asked the guy who was running things, Alan Fresco, who I'd be sharing with, he said Tom was 'a lovely fella, you'll get on great.'

But I'd never even met him and now I was sharing a room with him. I wasn't happy because I'm not the kind of bloke who's comfortable with strangers, I'd have much preferred to share with one of my pals. I shouldn't have worried. After a day I'd realise he was one of the nicest blokes I'd ever meet. A proper gentleman, who has now also sadly passed away.

By then I'd settled down and was really enjoying myself. The emotional separation from Jenny and the kids had slipped my mind. On the second or third day, at about six in the morning, we were in our beds and the phone rang. I just turned away and pretended to still be asleep. Tom, being a gent, answered it.

'Hello?' There was a pause. 'Andy, it's for you.'

'Who is it?' I said.

'Some woman.'

'Some woman at this time of the morning? What's going on?'

He gave me the phone and I said hello.

'So you're alive then.'

It was Jenny and she wasn't happy. She hadn't heard from me since I'd left and had hunted through the hotel numbers in the area trying to find me. When she asked why I hadn't phoned her I said the first thing that popped into my head, which was that I didn't know the international code. But I hadn't even tried to find the code. The truth was that everything had been such a rush I'd hardly had time to think. I'd gone to the airport and could hardly bear to say goodbye to her and the kids, but when I got to America I'd more or less forgotten them. That was terrible of me.

Over the years, I'd be away more and more. Sometimes I'd be in Holland for three weeks in one go. Being away from home catches up with you in the end; I wasn't really there to see the kids growing up. I'd come home and on the first day I'd be catching up with them, finding out what they'd been doing. Because I hadn't seen them for so long I wanted to make it up to them, so I'd give them 50 quid each whereas before they'd have got 50p. The next day I'd get a call and have to go here and there to see mates for various reasons,

47

and then the next thing I knew I'd be away again somewhere else for another tournament. I didn't really see them grow up at all. They were lucky to have a mum like Jenny. She was the one who brought them up, whereas I was just doing what I felt I had to do.

On my first trip away, once I'd apologised to Jenny I made sure I called her regularly. I had a great couple of weeks. We started off in LA, then went on to a town called Laughlan before hitting Las Vegas. Laughlan was right in the middle of the desert; at our hotel you paid $275 for four days and three nights and you were treated like VIPs. Food and drink were all paid for, the only time you put your hand in your pocket was for the odd dollar tip. I don't think it was the best idea they'd ever had to let darts players stay in a double room with a free bar at that price. They'd never seen anyone drink like we did.

At the time Bobby George was out in LA as well, so we met up with him when we arrived. He was doing an exhibition in Santa Monica, so Tom and I turned up at the pub where the exhibition was happening and eventually Bobby showed. Now, Bobby's well known for wearing all his gold and he made a big fuss as he came in – as he always does, he's Mr Here I Am. This woman said to him, 'Bobby, where's all your gold?'

He turned round and said, 'Do you think I'm going to wear it over here with all you thieving bastards around?'

I thought, *Nice one, Bobby, that's a good way to make friends.*

Bobby had a driver on that trip, an ex-American footballer who'd hurt his knee so he couldn't play anymore. His name was John Henry and he was massive – I mean *huge*, I'd never seen anyone so big. He was taking Bobby back to his hotel after the darts, so I asked if he'd give us a lift as well. In the car he looked ridiculous. Bobby's a big bloke but John was enormous – about 6'6", with legs the size of most people's bodies. He was so big he couldn't fit in properly, hanging out of the window on one side and onto Bobby on the other.

But he was a nice bloke, and on our way back he asked if we'd mind stopping off at his local to say hello to some of his mates. Bobby looked at me and I just said it was up to him. (I wouldn't have had the guts to say no to John anyway.) So in we went – me, Bobby and Tom. John said, 'Don't worry, whatever drinks we have I'll put on my card.' Then he ordered five beers, five shorts and some buffalo wings.

My maths isn't brilliant but I knew there were only four of us, which meant a spare beer. Just as I was wondering if he'd counted wrongly, I looked over and John necked one of the beers and then downed one of the shorts. Then he did the same with the other two. This carried on for about half an hour, by which time he must have had about 10 or 12 of them. He looked like he'd had a few, even for a big bloke. I told Bobby we were going to have to make a move soon because of the state of him.

Bobby said, 'Don't worry. Leave it to me.'

So we got back into the car. I don't usually like wearing seatbelts, but that night I'd have been happy to wear three because John's driving was terrifying. We sped off and swerved all over the place, close to the kerb, across the lanes. I was kicking the back of Bobby's chair, trying to get him to do something about it. Eventually he said, in his growling voice, 'John Henry, I've earned a lot of money in my life and I want to live to spend it. Now fucking slow down!'

After that John got a bit better, but I thought I'd remind

him how dangerous drunk driving is so I asked how he got on with the police over there. 'It's no problem,' he said. 'They do what they want to do and I do what I want to do.' I have no idea what that meant. Maybe he was just so big they left him alone.

We pulled up at the hotel, riding right up the kerb, and got out. We weren't going to argue with him. He was a lovely bloke, John Henry, but he couldn't drink for the life of him.

The first tournament in LA was blind draw pairs – where names are just pulled out of a hat – and I was beaten in the final. I played with an American in the first round. As Americans are usually quite loud, I had some mates there to support me. We started playing and, each time the American finished his three darts, he'd put his fist out towards me. I just nodded my head at him.

After a while I realised all the Americans were doing it – taking their throws and, no matter what they scored, touching fists with their partners on the way back. You see a lot of it nowadays, but at the time it was completely new. Being English, we wouldn't normally have dreamt of doing something like that. But as we were in America I thought I should be polite, so I thought, *Next time he comes back, I'll do that.*

The next tournament we went to, me and my mate Stevo paired up. We'd had a few drinks and decided to completely go for it, shouting and slapping each other's hands and really going over the top. I don't think people appreciated it very much but it made us laugh. That LA tournament was the best I did on that trip, losing in the final to Ronnie Baxter.

In Laughlan, I lost in the last 16 to Dennis Priestley and didn't do any good in the pairs. That tournament day was 24 hours of solid drinking. We stayed out as late as we could in the evening, had a few hours sleep and then got back on the beer at breakfast time.

I met some blokes who had become good mates of mine on that trip. There was Barry Nelson, Shane Burgess, Gary Robson and, of course, Stevo, or Dave Stephenson as I knew him back then. I'd met Stevo back in 1985, the year Raymond was born, through darts, but didn't see him enough to become proper mates until that American trip. We've been close ever since, for about 15 years now.

Those weeks in America were the first time I'd been away with Jocky Wilson, one of the biggest drinkers darts has ever known. Dennis was playing with Jocky in the pairs and, about halfway through the morning, went running around asking everyone if they'd seen Jocky. I asked what the matter was and he said he wanted to get hold of him before he had a few too many and spoiled his darts. No one had seen him, which we thought might be a good sign because it meant he wasn't at the bar with the rest of us.

Suddenly we heard this big, wobbly Scottish voice go, 'Ah, Dennis.' It was Jocky and he'd already had a few, although no one knew where. Dennis just looked miserable.

We went upstairs to play where there were lines of boards, with one board backing onto another. All you heard all day long was, 'Good darts, Dennis,' from Jocky, and I assumed he was having a laugh at Dennis's expense. But he wasn't. They were both playing well and they won the tournament. I was amazed.

What a character that man is. I loved Jocky. He's one of those people who just don't give a shit about anything other than darts and having a good time. And he was a *great* darts player, make no mistake.

We went from LA to Laughlan on a coach. It was 'the

bollocks' – massive, air-conditioned and with a fridge full of iced drinks. We even had two stewardesses, it was in a different class. We got there at one in the morning and the LA night air was like a hairdryer hitting you in the face. Obviously we had a few drinks when we got to the hotel.

We played the darts the next day and most of the lads we were with got beaten. Then someone told us there was a beauty contest round by the swimming pool, so me and Steve Beaton decided we'd go round and have a look, but when we got there it had finished. We were standing by the pool and one of the stewardesses from the bus was there with the bloke who owned the complex, so I said, 'Is it alright if we jump in and have a little muck around in the pool? With our clothes on?'

The bloke said, 'Fine, but take your shoes off and make sure you dry off before you go back into the casino.'

I just flicked off my shoes and was standing there ready to go. I turned round and there was Beaton – his shoes were coming off, his socks were coming off, his belt was coming off, his money was coming out.

'Your money's going to dry in seconds,' I joked, 'what's the matter with you?'

We stood next to each other by the pool and I said, 'After three. One, two ...' I put my hand on Steve's back and launched him straight in. As he went through the air all I heard was, 'You bastard!'

I got my shoes on quickly and was gone. I went through one casino, through the centre of the complex where they had a little miniature river, through the second casino and to my room. I locked the door and the next thing I heard was knocking. A few minutes later the phone rang. Then there was more knocking on the door. I hid for about two hours.

Eventually I got bored, went back out to the bar and saw Steve. He was furious.

I said, 'It's lucky I didn't go in.'

'Why?'

'I can't swim.'

I can, but I didn't tell him that until the trip home. It turned out that, when he was knocking on my door, he had a bucket of ice which he was going to throw all over my bed. It was lucky I didn't let him in, really.

They call Steve 'the Adonis'. He looks like Tom bloody Selleck, which means he stands out because there aren't many good-looking darts players. We did the Belgian Open once, where Steve's manager, Alan Critchlow, had arranged exhibitions for me and him. I bought two crates of Kronenburg to put in the motorhome, so when we got there we'd have something to drink. On the way we had a few beers and when we got there we had about eight left. Steve had about three more and I said it was his round.

'What do you mean?'

'I bought all those!' I told him.

So he went inside and got two drinks. We had those and he told me it was my round.

'No chance, I bought all those other ones. You've bought *one*. How can it be my round again?'

Steve is a great laugh and a lovely bloke, but he's murder when it comes to parting with his money.

On the way back, Steve had got a hotel room for him, me and Alan. When we got in there it had one double bed and one single bed. Steve was straight onto the single bed. I said to Alan, 'I don't know what you're doing, but you're not sleeping with me!'

I ended up lying there in all my clothes, wrapped up in a

blanket. Critchlow put his arm on me to wind me up during the night. I didn't like that at all.

After Laughlan we went on to Las Vegas and stayed in the Sahara Hotel. It was my first time there and I'd never seen anything like it. If you'd told me aliens created that city I'd have believed you. The place is in the middle of the desert and yet everything there – absolutely everything – is the best it can possibly be. I couldn't have imagined a place like it, it was amazing. But then there was the heat. Fuck me, the heat . . .

I even met Elvis, outside the Golden Nugget Casino. He's a little Chinese feller, about four-foot high, though he doesn't look like that on his album covers.

One day a few of us, including Bristow and Tom Kirby, went to a pool match. It was live on Sky and it was a nine-ball game. It was an important game, too, the World Cup or something like that. The Budweiser was about a dollar a bottle and some of us took full advantage of that. A Mexican chap was playing and doing pretty well. Bristow's quite good at pool and, after a while, he started giving the Mexican some banter, saying, 'I'll play you for 50 quid,' and all this while they were still playing.

I thought, *Fucking hell, Eric, this is going out live on Sky!* But we were in the audience and he was giving it out to them. He's a funny man, didn't care at all.

We drank so much that I don't remember getting back to the hotel room that night. (I know that I did, because that's where I woke up.) But Vegas was a great place, unlike anywhere I'd ever been before.

Back in LA, we did about four days in each place. When we flew back we went from Vegas to Chicago, then Chicago to Heathrow. At Chicago we were waiting for the flight when we heard an announcement that the plane had been overbooked. They wanted people to take some money to go on a later flight, but all I wanted to do was get home by then. We went up about three times, and eventually the guy said, 'I'm sorry to mess you around, but would you mind being upgraded?'

Well, of course we didn't mind being put up into business class, until we read the menu. I didn't know anything on there. I went to sleep and the next thing I knew someone was waking me up.

I heard this voice saying, 'Mr Fordham, Mr Fordham,' and I panicked.

I was half asleep and not thinking straight. Why the hell would they be waking me up? It must be an emergency. 'What?' I shouted.

'What would you like to eat?'

Eat? I thought there was something wrong with the plane.

I just pointed at something at the menu with no idea what I was asking for. All I got was a poxy little salad. I was starving when we landed back in London.

Jenny, the kids and my mum and dad were waiting for me when we got back. It was a great trip but it's hard to be away, even when you're off earning a living.

* * *

I've never liked travelling on planes and I've had some bad luck with them over the years. I was on my way back from Sweden once, after a darts tournament, and as we walked up the steps to board the plane the whole thing was shaking and moving around because the wind was blowing so hard. It was a nightmare. As we started taxiing out we were wobbling all over the place.

The captain started talking to us. 'Ladies and gentlemen, as you can tell, it's a little bit rough out there so what we're going to do is climb to 3,000 feet as quickly as we can to get above the bad weather. Hopefully once we're up there it will be a lot calmer and we can all have a nice, smooth flight.'

I was really nervous now. As we went along the runway, we were all thinking, *Fuck this for a laugh*. We all wanted to be out of there. Anywhere else would do. Off we went, down the runway, with the plane wobbling from side to side and shaking. Then, as we lifted up, there was a huge bang; the plane turned to one side and then to the other.

My mate Andy Jenkins was sitting away from me and started shouting, 'Fordy! Are you there?'

'What do you want?'

'This is the one, Fordy, we're going down! This is it!'

'Shut your mouth, you prick!'

Andy's a funny bloke and he usually cracks me up, but I did *not* find him funny that day. The next thing I knew, Chris Mason was smiling and saying, 'This is fantastic. What a great way to die!'

What the hell was wrong with these people? I was busy shitting myself and they were having a laugh. Luckily, we'd had a few drinks or I might have got *really* upset. (The flight was at about 11am, by the way. The drinking was just how we did things.)

We had another one in Finland. While the plane was waiting to take off someone noticed there was ice on the wing. As we were all looking out of the window, someone else piped up, 'Do you know the most common cause of air crashes?'

'No, what's that?'

'Ice on the wings.'

Why say things like that? *Why?*

One of the funniest flights was up to Scotland from City Airport. I got a taxi to the airport and then thought I'd better see which airline I was getting on. I pulled out my ticket and had to look at it twice: it said Suckling Airways. I'd never heard of them and suspected that Jeremy Beadle was going to pop out and start laughing at me any minute. But I looked up at the screen and Suckling Airways was up there, so I went along to check in.

I went through the airport to the runway to wait for the plane. When I saw it land it was like a minibus with wings, one of the smallest aircraft I'd ever seen in my life. I'm okay on the big planes – like the American Airlines flights where you get looked after – but the smaller ones are horrible. They might be just as safe and as quick, but I hate small planes. That flight felt like it took hours and hours, even though the weather was fine.

I used to fly from City Airport a fair bit. I call it Suicide Airport, because something always happens there to frighten the life out of me. One time we got on a flight to Holland with KLM. I used to be backwards and forwards there all the time, so I should have been used to it, but I wasn't. Our plane that day was one of those Focca 50's, a 50-seater. It was tiny, but still bigger than Suckling Airways' planes.

We were sitting on the KLM flight. The captain welcomed us aboard, started the engines up and was getting them going nice and loud. Then, suddenly, they died. All of them went off, just like that. But it was fine because we were still on the ground. Surely we could just get another plane?

But no, not at City Airport.

About five minutes the voice announced, 'Sorry about that, ladies and gentlemen, but one of our indicators is showing a faulty connection. What we're going to have to do is get you back into the airport while we arrange another plane for you. Apologies for the inconvenience and we hope to have you on your way as soon as possible.'

It was annoying, but at least they figured out the plane was dodgy while we were still on the ground. We were all getting ready to get off when the door opened and this bloke got on and opened the door to the captain's area to have a chat. Then he walked to the back of the plane where everyone gets on and off. He opened the door, then closed it a couple of times. Next he got a cloth out of his pocket and wiped the top, bottom and side of the door. Then he closed it, opened it, closed it and opened it again. He went in to see the captain, had another chat, turned round, got off the plane, shut the door behind him and the next thing I knew we were off.

I thought they were having a laugh. How could one bloke with a rag fix an entire plane? He could at least have got on with a toolbox to make it look right. I was shitting myself for the entire journey after that.

Luckily, there was a guy getting stuck in with his bird next to me and it took my mind off it, they really were going for it. That kind of behaviour isn't my cup of tea, but it was still a very pleasant distraction.

Of all the times I've been travelling through airports, I've only been pulled over by customs twice and they were two of the most embarrassing moments of my life. The first time, in 1994, I was entering America. At the time I was suffering with a bad back, and had been wearing a special corset to keep it straight. I had a spare one in my bag along with some cans of hairspray, which I use to keep my hair in place.

We were going through customs when this huge black

chap appeared and said to me, 'Excuse me, sir, can you come inside here?'

So in I went.

'Is this your bag?'

'Yes.'

'Can you open it?'

I started to go round to the other side of the table, because I couldn't open it from where I was.

'Get back!' he snapped at me.

'But I can't open it from here.'

'Get back!' he snapped again.

I was a bit scared now, because you don't want to mess with American customs and this chap was huge, so I turned the case round and opened it up.

'Is this your stuff?'

'Yes.'

Sure enough, out came a load of tins of hairspray followed by that fucking corset. This massive customs bloke held it up and started looking at me. I was blushing like a beetroot. He didn't move, just stared at me like I was some kind of freak.

Eventually I managed to speak.

'I've got a bad back, mate.'

He didn't say a word. He didn't have to. I don't know if he believed me but he let me go. Being a bit kinky isn't a crime, I suppose.

The only other time I was stopped was on my way back from Holland in 2001. It was for one night's work and the flight was leaving really early, so Jenny packed my bag for me the night before. I got up, gave her a little kiss and went on my way.

My mate met me at Schipol in Amsterdam and we went off and did the exhibition. We had a good night, a few beers, and when I got back to the hotel I thought I'd pack my stuff away so it was ready for the morning. I had my t-shirt and shirts hung up, then I got my pants out. But it was a pair of Jenny's knickers. I thought, *You silly cow, you've put the wrong ones in, now I'll have to go commando,* and that was the end of that.

The next morning, off I went. I was going through customs back at Gatwick, feeling a bit guilty. (I don't know why but I think everyone does, even when they haven't done anything wrong.) There were two women there in uniforms, one close to me as I went through and the other about 10 feet behind her. I had a feeling they were going to pull me over and the next thing I heard was, 'Excuse me sir, where have you flown from?'

'Holland.'

'Where, Schipol?'

'That's right.'

'Is this your luggage?'

I was getting nervous now and they probably noticed it.

'Yes, it's my luggage.'

'Have you got any other bags?'

'No.'

'Would you like to step over here?'

Oh fuck, I thought. As we walked over, the other woman went to the table so all three of us were there. Then the questions started.

'So this is your bag?'

'Yes.'

'You packed it yourself?'

'Yes.'

'Does everything in it belong to you?'

'Yes.'

I could hardly say my wife packed a pair of her knickers in there, could I?

She started taking my stuff out and, eventually, out came the knickers. I don't know if this is what customs people all around the world are trained to do, but she held them up and looked at me exactly like the American bloke did with the corset. But this time it was worse – it went on for ages. I didn't know where to look, I was so embarrassed. And it got even more embarrassing.

I used to go through customs at Gatwick quite a lot, and the blokes there would say hello to me and wish me luck for the darts. I don't know what happened this time but they must have all been in a room behind us, because they all came out laughing while she was holding up the knickers. As I said, I've never liked travelling on planes.

* * *

The first big tournament where I picked up ranking points was in Belgium in 1994. I went over there with a bloke who used to sponsor me. We got over there on the boat after drinking through the night, because it's difficult to sleep on a boat and there's nothing else to do. We left in the afternoon after I'd been in the pub from about midday, so by the time we got to Belgium the next morning I'd been drinking for the best part of a day and a half. That was normal behaviour for me.

We got to the tournament. I played one game and won it, but I didn't get called for another one for a few hours. My sponsor went up and asked why I wasn't playing anymore, and they said I was out of the tournament. 'Hang on,' he said, 'that can't be right!' It turned out that the bloke I'd beaten had played about four more games since he lost to me, but I hadn't played any because they'd made a mistake by calling the wrong person for the next round and he thought he'd got through instead. He'd then been knocked out by someone else, who was going to have to play me. I felt really sorry for this guy because he'd won some games and was making good progress in the tournament, but then had to come back and play me with his wins cancelled.

We played and I beat him. Fair play to this bloke, a Belgian called Rob, he supported me in every round after that. He was right behind me, though he was really pissed off with the organisers for messing things up for him. We've been friends ever since.

I got through to the final and played Rod Harrington, one of the best in the world, which represented a massive step up for me. I'd played Steve Brown in the semi-final and for the first time I was mixing it with the big names, people who'd been on the telly before I'd even dreamt about playing darts. Beating Steve was a special moment because it was the first time I'd won against a big name. I didn't beat Rod though, I wasn't good enough for that yet. He'd won the World Masters that year and was one of the top men. But I knew I could handle myself at that level and my confidence was up.

Before I played Steve Brown I wasn't expecting to beat him, but I never really go into a game expecting to win. I've always been the kind of player who takes each game as it comes, no matter who I'm playing against. In these tournaments funny things can happen. Sometimes you're better off playing someone you know well and come up against regularly, even if they have a higher rank than someone you've never played before, because you know what's coming. You know how quickly they play, how they look when they're feeling good or how frustrated they get if things start going against them. When it's a stranger, you have no idea what to expect and that can be very off-putting. Trying to read their emotions is impossible if you're only seeing them for the first time.

I'd played Rod earlier that year when he came down to a pub for a tournament. The guy who sponsored me at the time did the draw and pulled out my name to play against him in the first round. He said, 'Oh no, we can't have that,' and went to put my name back in. I had a right go at him and told him he couldn't do that. If he was going to do the draw he'd have to do it fairly, and that meant treating me like everyone else. He was worried because, as my financial backer, the man who paid for me to go to the tournaments, the further I went in the tournament the more he'd earn as he took a share of my winnings. Obviously, playing one of the best in the world in the first round wouldn't be good for my chances of going any further.

But I wasn't having any of it. You have to do these things properly and fairly, so I made sure the draw wasn't changed. I wouldn't have it any other way. Luckily, I won anyway, so my sponsor was happy.

In darts, every player has their own style. Some are similar but others stand out, like Dennis Priestley. He's a very slow player, noticeably slower than everyone else, which can cause some players problems when they come up against him. If he did it deliberately to wind people up then you'd have a right to complain about him, but he doesn't. It's just his way of doing things. But if you let it get to you, it can damage your game.

The first time I let something like that get to me was when I lost in the second round of the World Championships to

Marshall James in 1997. Marshall is a really slow player and it put me off my own game. Like Dennis, he doesn't do it deliberately to put you off, it's just how he is. A nice bloke who plays darts slowly.

Letting something like that affect how I played was rare for me. I could usually concentrate on my own game and not worry about how fast or slow the other guy was. Being quite a laidback character helps, I think. I'd be much more worried about playing Phil Taylor than a really slow or fast player, because it doesn't matter how slow or fast you throw your darts when your opponent scores like Phil does.

Everyone has their own pace which they're comfortable at. If you get drawn into playing at the opponent's speed then you lose that and you're not concentrating on what's important – getting your own game right and doing your own thing. I was always fine if I could play at my own speed, which is about medium pace.

The other thing about darts is that you play against your mates. I'd become good mates with Daryl Fitton when I played against him at the Lakeside the year I won it, and that was really hard. You really, really want to win, but it's difficult to be ruthless against someone you like and who you don't want to lose. That was one of the hardest games I've ever played.

My very first game in the Embassy was against Nicky Turner in 1995. We'd played together for years – pairs, Super League, county games, all sorts – so I knew him really well. That was difficult because I had the pressure of playing against a good mate, as well as the pressure of playing my first game at the World Championships. You have to put it out of your mind completely because it's easy to think, *Oh well, if I lose here it won't be too bad because my mate will go through instead of me.* If you think like that your head's gone and you'll be useless. It's easier to play against someone you really want to beat, someone you're not particularly good friends with. I've always preferred it that way.

Then again, playing someone you really dislike is hard too, because losing is that much more annoying. The ideal is somewhere in the middle!

* * *

When I started playing the occasional big tournament, at the end of the 1980s, I thought it was brilliant just being in the same hall as Eric Bristow because he was my absolute favourite player. One time, at a tournament in Stoke, I ended up standing near him at a bar and I was so excited I had to tell Jenny about it when I came out. She wasn't quite so impressed.

The first time I actually played Eric was in the early 1990s, at an exhibition at a pub near where I live now. I wasn't well-known then and I don't remember who won or lost, but I do remember very clearly in one leg throwing one hundred and something to leave myself an easy double to finish. As I was walking back he said, 'Good darts.' After that, I didn't care if I won or lost. Hearing that from Bristow was fantastic.

The better I got, the more big tournaments I went to. I started playing the better players and saw him around more. Eric was my idol and always will be. Some people don't like him, but for me the thing with him is what you see is what you get. If you don't like it, then hard luck, he won't change to impress people. I like him and we've always got on well.

These days, as a commentator on Sky, Eric is brilliant. Whether it's something natural in him which helps him understand players, I don't know, but he's almost always right. He can be talking about any player and nine times out of 10 he's spot-on. He'll say so-and-so is nervous, or so-and-so is up for this but struggling with his doubles, and then you'll see the player come out and his game will be exactly as Eric predicted. He's very intelligent about darts.

Eric was also spot-on in his assessment of me in his book. He says drinking pints is better for you than spirits, because the problem with shorts is that they are so easy to drink. Then he uses me as an example and, in his normal, no-nonsense way, he writes, 'With pints, you can only drink so many – unless you're Andy Fordham who used to drink 52 bottles of Pils in a session. Now he can't drink any more because he has been ill. Basically, he is knackered. If you're doing 52 bottles of Pils a night and you're on a ten-night tour, it's not going to do your body much good, is it?'

I can't argue with that. As usual he was bang on the money, no bullshit or messing about. That was a hard thing to read about myself but I didn't mind him writing it, because it's the truth. (And let's not forget it meant I got a mention in my idol's autobiography!)

I loved watching Eric play, not only because he was such a brilliant player but he had a great personality too, so cocky and entertaining. Whoever he was playing, he knew exactly how to wind them up. He'd do silly things like picking up the trophy and saying it would fit perfectly in the back of his car. He wouldn't just do it randomly, though. He'd know exactly who it would work with and who it wouldn't. Eric's a clever man.

It was a shame for everyone involved in the game, as well as his fans, when he developed dartitis – which is a very strange thing. I don't understand why it happens, but something psychologically occurs in a player's mind and he starts finding it hard to let go of his darts when he wants to throw them. He can stand outside and throw stones at a wall using exactly the same arm motion, but as soon as he comes indoors and throw darts instead he can't let them out of his hand. It's a terrible thing to happen. Eric was never the same player again, which was as big a shame for the game as it was for him because someone like him – who's a great personality as well as a truly brilliant player – is irreplaceable.

But he's still my idol. There's never been anyone else like Bristow. I saw old footage on TV the other day of him playing up in Scotland. He was playing Jocky Wilson so all the crowd were on his side and against Eric. Someone threw a can of beer at Eric, it whizzed past his head and hit the dartboard. It smashed open and there was beer everywhere, so they took him off stage. Apparently, backstage the officials were telling Eric he didn't have to go back on and play, but he said he would because if that lot couldn't hit him with a beer can he'd have nothing to worry about. He went back out there and was playing to the crowd, winding them up all in good spirits, he wasn't abusive.

When Eric played Jocky, you never knew what was going to happen because they were such great characters. I don't know if they were friends but I have heard Eric say he was glad he lost to Jocky in the World Championship final in 1989, because another win meant more to Jocky, who'd only got one before, than Eric, who had five. That's typical Bristow.

What Eric realised about darts before anyone else was how entertaining it could be. Eric knew how to entertain people. Playing that crowd up in Scotland, for example, he'd be making sure they got a good show and enjoyed themselves, which helped the profile of the game. Some people thought he was out of order when the Professional Darts Council broke away from the British Darts Organisation, but I'd never slag him off for it. He thought he was doing the right thing for himself and I respect that.

Around the time I first played Eric, I also met a lot of the players who had been my heroes when I started playing. Apart from Eric there was Bob Anderson, who was a great player and a nice guy, John Lowe, who I always found a bit strange, and then Big Cliff Lazarenko, who I bonded with because he was the biggest drinker around. He called me his 'little brother' once after a particularly big session, which was a compliment very few people ever received from him. He is great company, fun to be with and always enjoys himself. To me, that's what life is all about.

One time we were playing in Jersey and having a few drinks in the hotel bar late in the evening. For some reason, the guy running the bar decided to close it before we'd all finished, so Big Cliff took charge, buying two cases of wine – that's 24 bottles – and asking the barman to take all the corks out. He took all the lads up to his room, cleaned the bath out and poured all the wine in before telling the lads that if they wanted a drink they could just scoop it out. That's Big Cliff – everything he does is *big*.

Those were good times for me, but there was trouble brewing in darts. The split between the BDO and the PDC was just round the corner and would be a very bad time in the sport. In 1993 a group of BDO players decided to break away and form a new organisation which was going to put darts on Sky TV regularly, rather than just being on the BBC, and make the sport more professional with more money for the players. It meant that most of the top boys vanished from the BDO, because they thought they could do better financially by going to the PDC.

For me, that was a good thing. When all those players left I moved up the rankings, which meant I got into the World Championships sooner than I would have if they'd stayed. It's impossible to say how long it would have taken, but that progression definitely wouldn't have happened as quickly as it did.

Back in the early 1990s, I didn't really know how the system worked. I realised a few months after I started playing big tournaments that, if I'd carried on playing more tournaments, I've have picked up more ranking points and might have got to the Lakeside a few years before I did, even without the split between the BDO and the PDC. All I'd done until then was take each week as it came. The people who'd given me advice early in my career didn't know how it worked at the level where I was now, and I had no one advising me so long-term plans weren't really thought about.

For example, when I won my first big tournament in Finland, I followed it up by another one in Switzerland the following weekend. What I should have done is played the next one, and then the next one, as hard as I could to try to get myself further up the rankings. But I didn't. While I was away Jenny had gone down to Camber Sands on holiday with the kids and my mum and dad, and when I got back I went straight down to join them. I had a few quid in my pocket so we had a good week. But in terms of my career, I could have used that time better.

I never got involved in all the bad feelings between the two organisations back then. I had friends on both sides and my view was simply that the people who left did it for what they thought were good reasons, so good luck to them. You still hear different stories from different people about what went on, and who went behind whose back, but I don't want to know. I want to keep my friends on both sides of the fence and so have never criticised anyone.

I eventually moved to the PDC in 2009, simply because I wanted to play as many tournaments as possible as I needed the practice and the BDO don't play as often. No grudges, no fall-outs, nothing like that. All I wanted was to start making a living out of darts again and that seemed the best way to do it. If I'm going to get back to the highest standard possible, I need to play as much as possible.

Now I've joined the PDC, there are friends of mine from the BDO who will be as good as gold to me on the phone, but will start slagging me off behind my back. But I'm still not going to get involved.

FOUR

GETTING STUCK IN

After a few years of playing tournaments abroad, a kind of routine developed. Most of the time we would fly out quite late on a Friday and arrive at night, go straight to the hotel and try to get something to eat or have a few drinks if the bar was open. Whoever liked to have a drink before they played – and I was one of those players – would then be up at 6 or 6:30am the next morning to get a few down before the tournament began, which was usually at 10am. The drinking went on all day, which meant that if you did well and stayed in the tournament until the end you might still be playing at nine o'clock that night. You can imagine how much the players would have had to drink by then.

Not everybody would start drinking at 6am, but I was with a little crowd who did, like Andy Jenkins, Jason Thame, Colin Monk and a few others. We used to have a good laugh but we took our darts seriously. We were there to earn some money, pick up a few points and have some fun. After the tournament on Saturday we'd go out that night, usually to a restaurant or some people would go to a club. On Sunday you'd have the pairs competition, which wouldn't start so early. That meant you could get up a bit later, so I'd be in the bar at 7am. You'd play all day then, if you were still up for it, go for some food and a few drinks on Sunday night. Normally the flight back left quite early on Monday morning, so you'd be back home in bed by midday.

I used to share hotel rooms with Andy Jenkins a lot, and he became one of my best friends. He's a funny character too, a very amusing man, and absolutely nuts. People think I swear a lot but Andy really is Mr Tourette's. We were in Denmark once and were staying in a lovely hotel room. It was like a little flat – you went in from the corridor to a little hall, with a door on your left into the room with the beds and then another door in front of you to the bathroom, where the toilet and shower were. I got up one morning and went into the shower which only had a curtain, no solid door. I was washing myself when suddenly I heard a moan. I stopped what I was doing and thought, *What the hell was that?*

The noise stopped, so I thought nothing of it and started washing again. But then it came for a second time, longer and louder. I pulled the curtain back and there was Andy, sitting on the loo having a dump.

I asked him what he thought he was doing, but then I noticed something else. He'd left the bathroom door open and also opened the door to the hotel corridor, where there were people walking past. To make it worse, Andy the nutcase was saying good morning to everyone who went by – with him on the toilet and me in the shower.

As you might expect, I wasn't very happy about this. 'What's the matter with you?' I said. 'Are you some kind of lunatic?'

Andy smiled. 'Don't worry, it's alright. No one minds. It's good to be polite in the morning.'

'No it bloody isn't,' I said, and asked him to close the doors. He said okay, got up and went out of the bathroom, and I got on with my shower. I looked out again a couple of minutes later and he hadn't closed either door, so I had to get out of the shower in full view of anyone else staying at the hotel who happened to be passing along the corridor.

Thanks Andy.

I had some good times with George Noble, the referee who's now my brother-in-law after marrying Jenny's sister, Mandy. One day we were going to Holland by ferry. The crossing takes about six-and-a-half hours and there were a few of us on the boat over. We were all drinking quickly and most of us could handle it, but George is not the biggest drinker in the world so he was affected a bit more than anyone else.

After a while, he went to the casino. A few minutes later he came waddling back and said he'd lost all his money. He was going to get paid once we got to Holland, but he didn't have any cash left until then so he asked if I could lend him some.

'Not if you're going to go back in the casino, no way,' I said.

'No, I won't. I'm not going to.'

'You will,' I replied. 'I know you will.'

'I won't, honestly I won't.'

So I said, 'Fine, how much do you want?'

'50 quid.'

'What do you want that for?' I asked.

But George wouldn't tell me.

'Just give me 50 quid. I'll give it back to you when we get there.'

So I gave it to him. And then he did a stupid thing, as he does when he's pissed. From where we were sitting, the casino was off to the left. George went waddling off to the right, where there is a little corridor, thinking he was being clever. What he didn't know was that we could see into the casino from where we were sitting. We saw him walk in, sit at a table and put his money down. Then he had one go, shook his head, another go, shook his head again, and so on about 20 times. After that he came back and sat down.

'You've lost it all, haven't you?' I said.

'Yeah, I have.'

We had a few more drinks and George was pretty quiet. The water was like a sheet of ice that day so the ride was smooth and easy, one of the best crossings you could have. As we were talking, George was sitting to my left.

Or at least I thought he was.

I turned round to ask him a question and he wasn't there. I looked down and he was lying on his back on the floor, wriggling around trying to get up again like a turtle stuck on its back. He'd got so drunk that he managed to fall over on the calmest ferry crossing in history.

He's a funny character. Another day he stupidly decided he wanted to take me on at drinking. It was at one of the county games which happen once a month for nine months of the year, and his dad had come with us. I was playing for London against Essex. We went down there on a Saturday and George's old man said he wanted to have a drink, so we parked up at the hotel and got a cab to the venue. There was an A team game and a B team game; I was playing the A game on the Sunday, so I went along on the Saturday to support the B team.

George appeared next to me and said, 'Right, I'm drinking with you today. Whatever you drink, I'm drinking as well.'

I looked at him and said, 'Are you fucking stupid?'

'No, I reckon I can have a go. I'll be fine.'

So I said, 'Alright, fair enough. Let's see how it goes.'

We went to the venue. I asked George again if he was sure he wanted to do it. He said yes, so we went to the bar. I ordered a bottle of Pils and a bottle of Bud. It was just me and George drinking, because I'd asked George's dad if he wanted a drink and he wisely said something along the lines of, 'No, you idiots can fuck off. I'm not joining in with this.'

After about six bottles each, I ordered a bottle of Pils, a bottle of Bud and two brandies.

George said, 'I'll have Coke.'

'No,' I replied, 'you said you'd be drinking what I'm drinking.'

So he carried on drinking with me. Within three hours he was in such a state that he'd had a big row with his dad and pulled his trousers down in the middle of the bar, which wasn't bad for a shy bloke. Another hour and a half and that was him – the end of his day. We got a taxi back to our hotel. The taxi was white but, by the time we arrived, the paint on George's side was a very different colour. He was not very well the next day.

I was very lucky to be able to travel and work at the same time. It meant I could go to places I'd never otherwise have been to, like Norway, where I had one of the most bizarre experiences of my life. I went with Geoff Wylie, who used to organise tournaments and play them as well, and it was the first time that I met a lovely English lady called Anne Hoff, who lived out there and was really into darts.

We flew into Norway's main airport and then had to fly further up north to play an extra tournament. I can't remember the name of the town, but they paid for me to play in a competition which is why we travelled on. It was a blinding little place. We stayed in some darts fans' house and I had a great room downstairs with my own bathroom. It was lovely, they really looked after us.

We went out with them a couple of times and it's strange over there, because they don't go out in the same way that we do. Alcohol is really expensive in bars, so what they do is buy bottles of spirits and go to people's houses to drink there. We did all that and then, on the day of the competition, I started drinking at about nine o'clock in the morning as usual. The tournament didn't start until about midday and it went right round to the evening. I played Geoff in the final at about half past ten in the evening, and won.

Afterwards we all got into this big pink coach which was taking us back to the main tournament, the Norway Open, a journey of about 24 hours. I'd been drinking all day and on the coach. I started on what I thought was vodka with a mixer that looked like Tizer. Someone told me later it was cider, but I couldn't be sure. The stuff tasted good and that was enough.

I made it down to the main tournament the day after we left the other place, and I was out of it. I'd been drinking solidly for about 36 hours with about two hours' sleep in the middle and I was really pissed. At one point on the journey I woke up because I thought someone was trying to steal my shoes, when all they were really doing was taking them off to make me more comfortable!

On the way back down we hit a baby deer on the road. The mother went first as they crossed the road, but the coach just caught the baby behind her, the poor thing. The baby deer was definitely dead and, because they eat a lot of venison over there, the Norwegians we were with weren't going to let it go to waste. First they had to drain all the blood out of the carcass, because it goes poisonous after a while. They did that by the side of the road and then decided to give it to a guy whose father was a hunter and lived nearby, so he could have a barbecue with it later on. So off we went in this smart pink coach, turning onto a dirt track to get to this hunter's house. It must have looked ridiculous, this huge pink thing bumping along a track covered in potholes.

We got to this log cabin and the hunter came out. He looked like the real thing, old cap and grizzled face, like he'd been out in the woods killing animals for most of his life. He went round the back, got this baby deer, hung it up by its head and ripped it with a knife from the neck all the way down. Then he put one hand in by the neck and did some cutting with the other hand. Suddenly the baby deer's intestines came sliding out and he laid them out on the ground, metres and metres of them. It was only a baby but I couldn't believe how long they were, it was amazing.

Most of the blood had already drained out of the animal, but there was still some left. When we were about to leave the hunter came up and went to shake my hand. He still had blood all over his hands and I wouldn't have shaken them even if I hadn't been pissed. I just waved and got back in the coach as quickly as I could.

On the coach we started drinking again. The last thing I remember is being asked where the beer was by Roy Price, an English guy who runs a lot of the darts out in Norway, and telling him it was in the bidet. That's all I remember until the next day, when I was playing the tournament which I actually won.

I beat Andy Jenkins in the semi-final. Before the game he

spoke to his partner, Karen, who's a lovely girl, one of those really nice people who likes everybody. When he phoned her up and told her he was playing me in the semi, she said she didn't know who she wanted to win, which made me laugh. I can't remember who I beat in the final. It still amazes me now that I could play like I did with so much drink inside me.

I'm quite an emotional person and I'd had a really good time out there, so when I won the tournament I took everyone out for a drink. I think there were about 25 of us and we all had cider at about a fiver a pint, so it was quite expensive! The next day they gave me a present, a little statue, and I was really choked up. I had tears in my eyes. That was one of the best trips I ever went on.

I won the Norway Open again a couple of years later. This time we played on a big built-up stage. When we went to leave after the tournament, no one could find Chris Mason. After a bit of searching and shouting he came crawling out from underneath. He'd had so much to drink that he had to take himself off under the stage for a kip. He looked a right mess when he came out too.

After one of the tournaments, Anne Hoff took me and England captain Martin Adams out for a tour around some of the sights in the area. We went to a restaurant right next to one of the kind of ski jumps that Eddie the Eagle used to jump off. Because I'd never seen anything like it before, I wanted a closer look. I went and stood at the bottom of the bit where they take off, where it curves up. I looked up at where they took off from and thought it was a joke. How could they fly off something that high with just a pair of skis and a helmet?

Then I looked down at the bit where they land and it took

my breath away. I tell you, those guys must be mad! My respect for Eddie the Eagle went up so much that day. I know he wasn't very good compared to all the other ski jumpers in the Olympics, but he's a hero to me simply for having the balls to give it a go.

They told us we could go up to the very top and see the bit where the jumpers started off from, but I refused to in case I slipped. Imagine 25 stone of me sliding down that slope, out of control! Not a nice thought.

There was a simulator machine as well, and I wouldn't go on that either. Honestly, that thing looked terrifying! You see it on the telly and it looks quite impressive, but what you see on the screen doesn't give you anything like the full picture of what they're doing. Everyone knows that if you watch a game of football live it looks much quicker than when you see it on telly, and the same is true for the ski jump but on a different scale. I can't tell you how big those things are. It was unreal – I'd have been shitting myself if I'd just had to get all the way up and look down, let alone ski down it and jump. Fair play to Eddie the Eagle.

* * *

I played my first Embassy World Championship in 1995 and lost in the semi-final to Richie Burnett. But just being there gave me more of a profile, which helped me get invited to play exhibitions. The way exhibitions work is that a pub will pay a player to come in for the evening. They might get the brewery involved and give the player a couple of barrels, or get a sponsor involved. The player then turns up and spends the evening there, playing darts, talking to people and sometimes doing a question-and-answer session.

I'd usually get there at about six o'clock. You'd turn up, work out who you're going to play and then do the Q&A. The only things I wouldn't talk about were my kids or the split between the BDO and the PDC. People were always drinking and having a laugh, so they'd ask you anything at all. Someone once asked me if I was good in bed. I said, 'Of course I am, and I'm not one of those selfish blokes who goes on for ages either!'

A lot of players go to exhibitions and desperately don't want to lose when they play against punters. But to me it's not like that. Exhibitions are nights where people come to meet you and see what you're like as a normal person away from the stage. You do your work on the stage when you're playing the competitions. You go to the exhibitions to have fun and meet people. If I lost I wouldn't give a shit. In fact, I used to give people extra darts to help them win. They came along to enjoy themselves and I liked helping them do it. Losing every now and then didn't bother me at all.

If I got a good score, like a 180, I used to leave the darts in the board so the person playing me would get their score plus my 180. It was just a bit of fun, and as long as everyone was enjoying themselves I was happy. It's a great way to earn money and I'd love to do them again. I used to moan all the time about going to exhibitions, but once I got there I usually had a really good laugh.

I went to Wales with Richie Burnett to do an exhibition in his dad's pub. We were going to play a bit first and then do the questions after that. Now, I am known for swearing a lot and most of the time I don't even realise I'm doing it. So I said to Richie, 'You know I swear a lot, don't you?'

'Oh no,' Richie said in his Welsh accent, 'not in front of my mother!'

He was dead serious and I know Richie is a good boy who loves his mum, so I said I'd try to behave. We played the darts and then sat down to do the questions. I got the mic and said they could ask anything they wanted, but they had to understand that I swear a lot so they should please try not to be shocked. The whole hall went quiet. I thought, *Oh no, what's this going to be like?* So I said I'd try to leave out the naughty words.

When the questions had been going for a while, someone asked me if there were any darts players I didn't like. I said yes, there is one. They asked me who it was and I told them. Then they wanted to know what I really thought of him.

'I would tell you but I'm not allowed to swear, so I can't.'

'Come on, you can tell us!'

So I thought, *Fine, I will.*

'He's a fucking wanker.'

The hall went quiet again and I thought I'd really messed up. There were a few seconds of silence and then thankfully everyone started laughing. Even Richie's mum was fine about it.

As long as you don't go over the top and use the c-word, I think swearing is fine. I did a Q&A in a church hall once and there were kids everywhere. I didn't know how I'd manage but George told me I'd be fine. I got the mic and said to everyone, 'Now, I do swear a lot but there are kids here.' I'd had a few drinks by now, so I was feeling brave. 'But fuck them, they can hear it as well.'

Again, everyone laughed. That was lucky really, because someone could easily have got offended. Maybe I shouldn't have done it, but when people do swear there's a right way of doing it. I swear as I talk normally, I don't do it aggressively, it just comes out in the flow of what I'm saying. I often don't mean to do it either, which is why I've sworn on live TV before. I was doing an interview with RTL4 in Holland once and talking about a BDO vs. PDC tournament. Someone said something about a player who'd done well and I responded, 'Of course he did well, he's a fucking good player.' No one said a word. They just carried on with the interview as if I'd said nothing out of the ordinary.

The next night, I was lying in bed half-asleep with the telly on. Wayne Mardle had just lost to Co Stompe, but Co couldn't do an interview because the tournament was on RTL4 and he was contracted to SBS6, a different channel. Wayne came out on his own and they asked him, 'What happened?'

'Well, I was fucking shit, wasn't I?'

I woke up then. Did he really say what I think he said? Next question.

'So you're not happy then?'

'No, I'm not fucking happy. I played like a plonker. I was fucking shit.'

Yes, he *did* say what I thought he said. Wayne carried on swearing about a few more things, then he stopped and said, 'Don't you want to hold back some of these questions for when Co gets here?'

'No, Co's not coming,' the producer said. 'This is the only interview. And it's live.'

Wayne's face went white. He was mortified.

'I'm so sorry, I didn't know it was live. I'm so sorry for swearing like that.'

Poor Wayne. How was he to know? The guy should have told him from the start, but it was fucking this and bollocks that all the way through. I think at one point the interviewer asked Wayne how Co played and he said, 'He was fucking shit too, just not as fucking shit as I was.'

Luckily, I've never let it all out quite as badly as that.

FIVE

FAR AND WIDE

Over my years playing darts I've met so many lovely people that I could write another book about them all, especially those who've looked after me as I've travelled around. I've been to some brilliant places, countries I would never have been able to visit if it hadn't been for darts, so I think I've been very lucky.

In the early 90's, the one thing I said I wouldn't do was go to Northern Ireland because of the Troubles there. But Jenny's family are Irish and they said it would be fine, so I agreed to a trip. The fact that I'm a Rangers fan didn't worry me because people didn't know about it at that stage, as I hadn't broken through to televised games yet. It was more about being scared of the place and what might happen to me when people found out I was English. I'm not massively into politics, but all the papers seemed to write about was people being killed.

I now know I was worrying far more than I needed to, but at the time I really didn't like the idea of going into a possibly dangerous area where I didn't know my way around and didn't have many friends. In the end, my first time over there was awkward for a very different and thankfully far less dangerous reason.

It was Geoff Wylie who persuaded me to go over. Geoff was one of Ireland's top players who'd moved onto organising exhibitions. He'd invited me over before but I'd always said no. This time things had changed. It was 1995 and I'd just reached my first semi-final at the Lakeside. Getting that far in the World Championships made your name bigger and increased your value for exhibitions, so I started doing more. Geoff said I could earn £1,500 for going over and playing one or two matches in Northern Ireland. That was a lot of money to me at the time – it still is, actually – so I went. I played the German Open, flew back to England and then straight out again to Northern Ireland.

At the time I didn't eat very much at all because I was drinking constantly. I was taking in so much liquid that I didn't have space for anything else. Given the choice between food and alcohol, I'd pretty much always go for alcohol. I only drank downstairs in our pub, not upstairs in our home, and Jenny reckons I was getting through 10 crates of beer a week – that's 240 bottles – because if I wasn't away playing darts and drinking I was playing darts in our pub and drinking. I don't know why, but I never seemed drunk or like I had a hangover, which meant the drinking didn't affect my darts.

If I did eat it would be late at night after a lot of booze, and even then it wasn't much. When I met Jenny I had a 28-inch waist and at my biggest, 28 years later, I wore a size 56. Imagine how much bigger I'd have got if I ate as well!

But I didn't have an appetite for food while I was drinking, and so on the plane over to Northern Ireland all I had was a sandwich. I didn't want any more food because I was full. We got into the airport and I was a little bit on edge, because I didn't know what kind of atmosphere I was walking into. I met up with Geoff, we got in his car and went on our way. It was all fine. I began to relax a bit.

Then he piped up, 'Andy, are you hungry?'

'No, I'm alright, thanks.'

'Are you sure? You should probably have something to eat.'

'I had something on the plane, I'm fine.'

'Okay, I'll do you a fry.'

I had a fair idea of what he meant by a fry, and I do have a soft spot for them. I just didn't want one that day.

'I don't want a fry, Geoff. I had something on the plane and I'm not hungry.'

'Okay, I'll get Anne to do you a small one.'

'Geoff, I don't even want a small one. I'm not hungry.'

By then he was already on the phone to Anne, his missus, telling her we'd be home in 15 minutes and to get started on my food.

'Geoff, I'm not –'

He cut me off. 'You're having a small fry.'

I wasn't even given a choice, even though I really didn't want anything to eat. So we got to their house in Ballymena and I met Anne for the first time. I wanted to make a good impression because Geoff's a good pal, so I tried to be a good guest.

Anne is a lovely lady and I've got on brilliantly with her ever since. But that day was awkward because, after a couple of minutes, out came my 'small fry'. There were about four pieces of bacon, three sausages, eggs, mushrooms, tomatoes, and then there was the bread – which, over there, means potato bread, soda bread, normal bread, toast. I thought, *Small fry? You're having a laugh!*

I looked at Anne and said, 'I can't eat all this!'

'Don't you worry, Andy,' she said. 'Eat as much as you want and leave the rest. That's fine.'

So I started in on this huge plate of food. I really tried to put away as much as I could, but then started struggling and getting a bit sore in the stomach area, because I wasn't used to eating this much. I told Anne I was really sorry but I couldn't eat any more. I felt terrible, because she'd gone to all that effort and I must have left enough food on that plate to feed me for about three days.

Then she took away my plate and threw the whole lot in the bin. I thought I'd offended her really badly, but actually that's just the way the Irish are – so generous to everyone. I've got used to it over the years, but that first time was quite a shock. I'd been worried about coming to Northern Ireland because I thought it would be dangerous, but I didn't think the danger would come from overeating!

Geoff and I then headed off to the exhibition. I was shitting myself again now, because meeting a room full of strangers over there was what I had been most scared of. But the people were brilliant, so very friendly, and I had such a laugh. After that night I said to Geoff, 'I will come over here any time, any time at all.' I had an amazing week and the people were so nice it seemed unreal.

On the last night we were driving off to the exhibition, heading out of the town and into the countryside. After a while I realised it had been about half an hour since I last saw a house or any kind of building, and I started to get a bit worried because there was nothing but fields for miles around.

Finally, we got to a pub standing in the middle of one of these fields, bang in the middle of nowhere, and all there was outside was a tractor, a trailer and a pushbike. I thought, *Blimey, there won't be many people out here tonight!* But we opened the door and it was rammed. I had no idea how they managed to fit all those people in there because it was absolutely packed, people were jammed in everywhere. Where the hell had they all come from? I didn't have a clue, it made no sense at all.

It was another great night, although, right near the end, after the exhibition had finished and we were all having a few drinks, I had my first taste of the less friendly side of the place.

I was at the bar and a guy came up to me with a look in his eyes I didn't like. 'So, what football team do you support?'

I didn't know what to say to that. I didn't know if I should say the truth or what difference being English would make. Luckily, one of his mates stepped in and said, 'No, no. Don't say that. We don't talk like that anymore, that's all history,' and he walked off. I thought, *Thank God for that.* That was the only time anything like that happened. I went out there a few times after that and loved it. I became good mates with some of Geoff's friends and used to really enjoy my visits.

On another visit, I was on my way to an exhibition with Geoff and we saw this bloke hitchhiking. Geoff, being as friendly and generous as everyone seems to be over there, said, 'I wonder where he's going. We could give him a lift.'

I was still as nervous as hell over there, so I replied, 'Could we bollocks! We are not giving him a lift, you have no idea who he is!'

But Geoff ignored me and we picked him up. This stranger

was sitting behind me and I was all over the place. All the stories I'd heard about terrible things happening came flooding back to me. I was not comfortable.

After a while the guy figured out who we were, got a bit excited and phoned up his local pub to tell them he was with us. We drove for about 20 minutes, got to the pub he was going to and he asked us to come in to meet his friends and have a drink – just one. But it's never just one drink over there, not when the people are as nice as they are. So we were in there for about an hour and a half, even though we were on our way to an exhibition. We were late for it but no one minded. They're a different class.

At one exhibition at another pub, it got to about 9pm and we were all still talking and drinking. Now, I usually like to start between 8 and 8:30pm to give me plenty of time to play all the people who want a game. But that night at 9pm there was still nothing happening, so I asked Geoff to get the names of everyone who wanted a go. Half an hour later he hadn't done anything, so I asked him again. It wasn't until about 11:30pm that he finally got them and we started playing. I was well on the way by then and we didn't finish the darts until gone 2am. What a great night!

And it didn't end there. When it finished, Geoff came up to me and said the landlord had asked if I wanted something to eat. I said yes please, and the next thing I knew everyone was putting on their coats. I thought they'd changed their minds and we were going home, but we all trooped off to this Chinese restaurant. There must have been 16 of us around the table, all tanked up. We'd just sat down when the waiters brought out these jugs of water.

I turned to Geoff. 'Water? I don't want water. What's this all about?'

'Don't worry,' Geoff said quietly, 'this place isn't licensed. Just have some.'

So I did. It was wine, but served up in jugs so that if you looked in from the outside it looked like we were drinking water. It was very clever and very effective too, because we drank a lot of jugs of wine long into the night.

My visits to Northern Ireland showed me you shouldn't judge people or places until you see them for yourself, because I loved my time over there and I loved the people. I knew the place had its problems but they weren't anything to do with me. As I said earlier, I'm no politician.

At first I loved all the travelling. I hadn't been abroad much before and it was exciting, particularly as it meant my darts career was taking off. As you go higher up the ladder you play more and more tournaments and more darts fans want you to play exhibitions. But it's tiring, because you're not on holiday when you go away as a darts player. People think you go to all these different countries and see so much of the places, but you don't. If you're lucky and do an exhibition or two first you'll be travelling around a bit beforehand, but if you're just there for the tournament you don't see anything except the airport, the hotel, the dartboard and the bars. Don't get me wrong, it was great fun and I'm not complaining. But it's probably true that travelling as a darts player is more like a business trip with your mates in tow than a holiday.

They weren't all brilliant, though. Every now and then I'd have a bad experience. I did one in Holland after I'd won the Embassy, and when we got to the event there were TV cameras and everything outside. I heard from inside the place, over the loudspeaker, 'Ladies and gentlemen, please welcome World Champion Andy Fordham!'

Straight after it they started playing 'I'm Too Sexy' by Right Said Fred. I was really embarrassed when I had to walk in to that. I had to walk up four flights of stairs and as you went into the bar there was another room next to it; there were about 400 people in each section and those in the separate room had paid money just to be able to watch the exhibition on a TV screen. It was madness – great fun, but absolute madness.

That kind of thing would frighten the life out of me now, facing all those people who'd come along especially to see me. Most of the time people were well-behaved, but every now and then there would be a prat. I did one in a big hall once where there was a little stage made up. Everyone was standing below and we were up there playing. It was all going fine when this guy came up to play me and shook my hand before we started our match. Then he said, 'If I win, I can have your wife.'

I didn't really react to that. I didn't think it was funny either, mind you, just not worth kicking up a fuss about. But a bit later, he turned round and said, 'And I can have your daughter as well.'

I tried my bollocks off after that because I wanted to thrash him. And I did. After the game he stuck his hand out. I grabbed it and pulled him right up close to me and said, 'If you talk about my family again, I'll throw you off this stage. Now fuck off!'

There were about 10 blokes there who were acting as minders for me because the place was packed. They could see something was up so they asked if I wanted a break. I said yes, and someone asked what the matter was. I pointed at the guy and said, 'Just keep that fucker away from me!'

This guy kept trying to come over to apologise for what he

said, but I wasn't having any of it. Eventually they chucked him out. I didn't feel sorry for him because he shouldn't have said it in the first place. He was lucky I didn't punch him right on the nose.

I'm not a violent person, by the way. I've never been a fighter. But I've come close to whacking someone at darts a few times, and it's almost always been when someone has talked about my family. At last year's 2008 Dutch Open I went along to see my pals play and support them. One night I went for a Chinese with a few of them and, because the food was taking ages, I got the hump and left. I was never like that before I got ill and stopped drinking, but I guess that's what going off the alcohol after so long does to you – it changes your character a bit.

I left the restaurant and went to a bar to wait for the others to come along. There were a few players and some mates. We were there drinking (lemonade in my case) and having a chat when, out of the blue, this guy came up to me and said, 'How old is your daughter?'

I stood there and went all quiet. 'Why the fuck would you want to know that?'

'Well, I'm just –'

I cut him off. 'Why? Just leave me alone.'

Why would he come up with that? It totally ruined my night. I didn't want to talk to anyone for the rest of the evening.

Something similar happened again when I went to Brighton in early 2009 for the Premier League with Jenny and Stevo. We got to the venue and someone spotted me, so it started straight away, people wanting photographs, autographs, all the usual. As I've said before, I really don't mind doing this kind of thing. But every now and then a dickhead comes along who spoils it for everyone. There were about six stairs up to another part of the venue. I was standing at the bottom having pictures done and Jenny was at the top waiting for me. This bloke had his picture taken with me and then said to Jenny, 'You know, I wouldn't mind having my picture taken with his daughter as well,' and then laughed.

She went, 'Oh really?'

'Yes, she's lovely.'

'Well, I wouldn't let him hear you say those things because he doesn't take too kindly to people talking like that about his daughter.'

'Really? How do you know?'

'Because I'm the mother of that daughter and I don't like it either.'

The guy went bright red and ran away. What a prick! There's no excuse for behaving like that, and to say it to the girl's mum is pretty stupid.

Before I give the wrong impression, the bit of trouble I had in Holland was a one-off. Every other single time I've been there I absolutely loved the place. It is amazing. The Dutch are mad about their darts and the players are celebrities in a different way to over here. We got much more attention and had some serious fans. Some people don't like that, but it didn't bother me. I mean, we used to get asked to sign boobs and arses all the time, which isn't exactly a chore. But getting your signature right in those situations can be quite tricky if the arse is a bit wobbly, so you have to hold it steady to write. It's a tough life, being a darts player.

(I'm not being sleazy, by the way. Jenny knows all that stuff goes on and she knows that things like that are just a bit of fun.)

One night I was at a tournament with Russ Bray and we

were sitting on the stage before we started playing. A girl came up to us – not old but not particularly young either – and got her tits out for us to sign, which we did. Then another girl came up, about 19 or 20 and lovely looking. She lifted up her top for us to sign her belly and everyone around us started booing because she hadn't got her tits out as well. The girl put her hand up to get everyone quiet, turned round, undid her trousers, pulled them down and bent over. She had a tiny white thong on and, well, that's a picture that none of us will forget for a while.

For some reason, things like that seem to come more naturally to the Dutch than the British. Maybe that's why they're so laidback and friendly – everyone's happy to take their clothes off. I had some great, great times with them and it's one of the nicest countries I've ever been to.

There are some really good Dutch players as well, like Co Stompe, Jelle Klaasen and Roland Scholten. I first met Roland when we were going to America to play back in the 90's. We were in the same group and must all have been talking for two hours when someone said something in Dutch. Roland replied in good Dutch and I asked him where he learned it. He looked at me like I was an idiot.

I said, 'Why are you looking at me like that?'

'Because I am Dutch.'

I couldn't believe it because his English was absolutely perfect. How many English people can speak Dutch to that standard? (Probably none.) Roland is a really nice bloke and a good player too.

The Dutch were always great to me. One of my favourite memories of what the people are like comes from when I was over there playing on February 1, the day before my birthday, early in the 2000's. We'd played that night and were having a few drinks so things were getting loud and rowdy. But the clocks got to midnight and it all stopped. Someone got the mic out and started talking to the crowd. They were speaking Dutch but he was translating for me, so I knew what they were saying. They started singing 'Happy Birthday' in Dutch and then told me they had a present for me. I'm not being ungrateful but I've been given loads of things over the years, usually bottles of drink, so I wasn't getting all that excited.

But there was something with a cover standing close to us. It was a few feet high and had a round end. I had no idea what it was. Then someone said, 'Here's your present,' and took the cover off. It was a birdcage with a budgie in it. That was one hell of a surprise.

I used to have budgies when I was younger but I hadn't done so for years, so I have no idea how they found out I liked them. The trouble was, even though it was a lovely present and all that, I was flying home the next day and there was no way I could take it on the plane with me. But I also couldn't say, 'Thanks but no thanks,' after all the effort they'd gone to. Luckily, the woman who runs all the exhibitions over there, Suzanne, took it to her house and kept it there. She took quite a shine to the bird in the end and bought it a friend so it would have company.

They always make me smile, the Dutch. For a while, darts was so massive over there that the organisers would need a lot of help for the exhibitions because the events were so huge. They would need stewards, security, it wasn't like filling up a pub over here, it was huge, with hundreds and hundreds of people. As a thank-you to the people who worked at the event, the organisers would put on a meal for them before or after the exhibition. It also gave them a chance to meet the player and was a nice touch. I had such a good laugh at those things and met some great people – Big Frank Penders, who runs a darts shop, for example, and Jules, who has a bar. I used to see these people all the time, but since I got ill I haven't been over so much, which is a shame. I hope I'll be back over there again soon because I'd love to see them again.

We used to stay in Germany in a place called Emlichheim right by the border and then go across into Holland to a place called Coeverden and a bar called Café de Port, which was run by a Dutch couple, Albert and Angelique. Albert had a lovely Alsatian dog called Bolo and used to call himself King Bolo. He'd dress up in lederhosen all the time and used to make me laugh so much. They were so friendly and whenever I was over there and had a night off – which used to happen every now and then, as I'd often stay for two or three weeks – I'd be straight down to their bar to see them. Sometimes other darts players would get annoyed with me because I'd always go over there to see Albert and Angelique, but I went anyway. I loved going there, I felt so welcome; I made friends with the regulars and we'd all play cards together. They were all lovely people and great fun.

One time when we went over there we went on a plane which could take off and land on water or on land, and which was used in the Second World War to sink U-boats. We were filming with SBS6 and they told us they had a surprise for us. They took us to this lake, with no mention of planes or flying; I took one look at this thing – it was called a Catalina G-PBYA – and said, 'No chance, I'm not getting in that.' Eventually they persuaded me and I squeezed myself into this thing through a tiny door. I sat down and tried to do up my seatbelt. Of course, me being the size I was, it wouldn't go round me. One of the girls went off to look for something they could use to help strap me in; she came back with something, hooked it in and when I breathed out it snapped. Finally, she got a belt from another chair and tied it in a knot around me. Before I could say anything we were off and I was stuck in this seat.

We went up and flew over the lake to see how rough it was. Then we came back and down onto the water, landing like a speedboat. They told us we were allowed to stand up and look out to get the best view, but I was tied to my chair so I couldn't move! I was so nervous I don't think I'd have stood up anyway. SBS6 filmed it all but I never saw it – which was probably for the best as it might have been quite embarrassing.

You don't just meet darts players at tournaments and events, there are also other people who you become mates with, like my pal Tiger Carroll. I met Tiger at a Courage beer event in Essex. I got there and the bloke who arranged it all introduced me to everyone. There was a tribute band to The Who, so I asked if they wanted a drink.

They said, 'Oh no, we don't drink.'

'You're a tribute band to The Who and you don't drink? You must be joking.' I was not impressed.

The next few I met weren't drinking either, which was giving me the hump as I wanted someone to have a few beers with me. Then along came Tiger. His real name is Bernard and he's a Maori, he has tribal tattoos down both sides of his head, each side the exact mirror image of the other. He's a walking work of art.

Tiger said hello and I asked if he wanted a drink. He said, 'Yes, a JD and Coke please,' and I thought, 'Right, you'll do for me.' I was pleased because I had someone to drink with, and luckily we got on well. In fact we became really good friends straight away and have kept in touch ever since.

Tiger came to the darts a few years later and everyone was being really nice to him. Malcolm Kemp, who was filming it for the BBC, is a Kiwi too so they had a really good chat. Later I introduced him to Bobby George. All day, everyone had been going on about Tiger's tattoos and how much they must have hurt but, Bobby being Bobby, he had to be different. He started rubbing Tiger's head and said, 'Did you paint them on this morning?' I thought, *Oh dear, here we go*, because Tiger is a hard bastard. He used to play rugby league for London Broncos and is not that tall, but he's as big and solid across the chest as anyone I've ever met. He's a very strong, tough man, and I thought he was going to get the hump big-time with Bobby.

Tiger looked at him and said, 'Yeah, Bobby, that's right. And I've done one for you as well.'

'Oh yeah, what's that?'

Tiger folded his bottom lip over and showed Bobby the letters tattooed on the inside of his mouth, spelling out, 'YOU C**T.'

There wasn't much Bobby could say to that, so he just grunted and walked away while we all laughed.

I went out with Tiger a good few times after that. He used to come down to the pub to be a judge for things like karaoke competitions, he'd turn up on his Harley Davidson, looking the business. He's a hard man but he's one of the nicest blokes you'll ever meet, a complete one-off.

The main darts circuit is great because of where you go and the people you meet. But I loved the smaller tournaments as well, and if I had to pick my favourite it would have to be the Portland Open at the Portland Club in Inverness, up in Scotland. It's run by my now very good friend, Gordon Morrison, and I loved it every time I went there. That may have something to do with my record – I played my first one back in 1995, and it was the first time I'd won both the singles and the pairs at the same tournament; I then did the same again in 1996. It was my lucky venue!

Everything up there is brilliant. The first time we went we stayed at the Kessock Hotel which is run by Cilla and Dennis Maclachlan, along with their sons Derek and Darren, lovely people who just can't do enough for you. Gordie's mum and dad, Ian and Heather, were the same, I always felt welcome with them. The fact that the Portland Club was a Rangers club helped too.

At the Kessock they had this boat which held about 12 people and they used to take people out on it. On the day of my first singles we all got on the boat and went from the hotel across the Moray Firth to the Portland Club. We saw dolphins and seals on the way, which was just incredible. As I walked down the ramp to the boat, I slipped and fell to my knees with two bottles of beer in my hands – being me, I managed not to spill so much as a drop!

After a couple of years of my going up there, Gordie started to arrange exhibitions for me and one night his brother-in-law drove me to one. We borrowed Gordie's very nice BMW for the journey with its white leather seats. As normal, I was drinking my bottles of Pils as fast as I could, but I had nowhere to put the empties. At the time the backseat seemed like a good place to leave them, but it wasn't such a clever plan as Gordie didn't let us use his car again when he found out!

The next time we had a long trip we borrowed another car. Martin Fitzmaurice and I were driven all the way down from Inverness to Dumfries by a lovely bloke called Sam; I don't remember the details so well, but he reckons I drank nearly a case of Pils on the way – that's almost 24 bottles. When we got to the exhibition venue they said they didn't sell Pils. I wasn't happy, so I told them I wasn't playing without any of the beer I liked. After that, they sent someone to the local off licence and all was okay.

I still feel bad about that. Everyone up there used to make me feel so welcome and I had some great times. A big thank-you to them all and apologies for my behaviour that night!

SIX

THE WORST
OF TIMES

At the end of 1989, Jenny was working as a receptionist for Asda in Charlton, I was a store man at Tobacco Dock and Raymond and Emily were four and three. One morning, while she was in the shower, Jenny felt a small apple-pip-sized lump on the side of her left breast. It moved up and down about half an inch either way, but she ignored it at first because she had to sort the kids out for the day and get to work.

Later that day, while she was at work, Jenny couldn't get the lump off her mind and mentioned it to a friend, who said she should see a doctor. She made an appointment for the next day. My mum went to pick her up from work later with the kids and she told her about it straight away. Then, when I got home, she told me too. I was very worried and said I would go with her to the GP, but Jenny said there was no point in both of us going because, at that stage, she didn't think it was anything serious.

Jenny saw her GP the next day. He examined her and said he didn't think it was anything to worry about but, to put her mind at rest, he would send her to a breast screening clinic at Guy's Hospital in London. The appointment with the consultant came through in only a couple of weeks, which worried us a bit as we all knew how long it took to get to the top of hospital waiting lists in those days.

I went with Jenny to see the consultant and the hospital was amazing – it was much bigger than those we'd been to before and we couldn't believe how many people were there. Before she was examined Jenny had to fill out a long medical history form, which was very boring as nearly all the answers were 'no' because she'd always been very healthy. She went in to see a doctor who looked at the lump, poked it and said to her, 'It's what is known as a breast mouse. It's nothing to worry about and we can remove it, but as you are so young you won't want a big, ugly scar so we should probably leave it.'

Jenny didn't want a scar and if the lump was doing no harm, we both thought, *Why interfere?* So we went home and told everyone it was nothing serious. The lump didn't go away and still moved around, but she was fine with it.

A few years later Jenny noticed the lump had grown to the size of a pea, but it still moved around. She thought about going to the doctor but figured she would probably get the same diagnosis as before, so she decided not to waste the GP's time and left it. Within a few weeks it was the size of a large gobstopper and had stopped moving. She went back to her GP, who took one look and told her to take a letter by hand straight to the breast clinic at Greenwich Hospital. She did that and was given an appointment very quickly.

This time she went on her own as we were still not too

worried. The lump had been there for a while, so we thought that if it was going to be anything serious we would have known by now. Jenny got to the hospital, was called into the examination room and told to remove her upper garments. The consultant would be along shortly. About 15 minutes later, in walked an old-ish man with grey, receding hair and half-rimmed gold glasses on the end of his nose. He had Jenny's notes in his hand, stood in front of her and asked, 'What's the problem?'

She pointed to the lump, describing how it was now static and much bigger than before. He leaned forward and said, 'It's not even in your breast, woman,' waved her off with his hand and left. Jenny sat there for a few minutes feeling bemused and stupid. She was glad she hadn't worried anyone with her terrible fears, as she was obviously wasting the doctors' time. We both put it out of our minds. After all, if they didn't think there was anything to worry about, why worry?

That was it until 1997. By then we were running the Queen's Arms pub in Woolwich and my darts career was taking off. I'd been on TV in the World Championships a couple of times and I was becoming quite well-known. We'd even appeared on *Through the Keyhole*, which was a very funny experience. A camera crew came and looked round our house and then we were driven up to Leeds to the studio, where we met Sir David Frost. They gave us loads of beers on the way up and a £500 fee too. Not bad at all.

All was going well when, after a really bad bout of tonsillitis, Jenny was sent to have her tonsils removed. The operation was booked for August that year. But she was quite a heavy smoker at the time and, about a week before the operation, cancelled the surgery due to a chest infection.

Jenny's doctor sent through a new date for December and she went to her GP for antibiotics two weeks before, just to be on the safe side as she didn't want to put it off again. Her GP was on holiday so she saw a locum, who was very nice and understanding about her fears relating to smoking and the anaesthetic. She listened to Jenny's chest and said it was fine, but asked if she knew that she had an abnormal growth in her left breast.

Jenny went through the whole story of what had happened with it, and told the doctor it was fine. But the doctor shook her head and asked if she had ever heard of breast cancer, writing her a letter to take to the breast clinic. Jenny had her tonsils removed on December 9 and went to the clinic on the 18th, where she saw a very nice consultant called Mr Montgomery. He examined her and said he was sure it was okay, but took a sample of the fluid from inside the growth anyway and booked her to have it removed on January 11. He wanted to make absolutely sure it was okay. She left feeling relieved. Finally it would be sorted out, and she felt at last like the doctors really cared.

Christmas came and went and we were very busy at the pub, while I was getting ready for the World Championships in January. On the morning of New Year's Eve, Jenny opened the pub and was getting ready to go shopping for food as her dad, sisters and their husbands and children were all coming over to celebrate New Year. She was in the middle of it all when she got a phone call from the breast nurse at the hospital, asking her to go and see Mr Montgomery that afternoon as he wanted to talk over a few things before the operation. Jenny said she couldn't get there until about 3pm as she had to do the shopping first. Her sister, Sally, went with her to the hospital. As they sat in the waiting room, laughing and chatting and looking forward to the evening, they hoped they wouldn't be at the hospital too long because there was more shopping to do and a dinner to cook.

Then they were taken into Mr Montgomery's room, where he sat them down and told Jenny it was cancer.

Sally's knees buckled. Because Jenny didn't react, the doctor wasn't sure if he'd told the right person. Jenny had no idea she was going to be told she had cancer, and so she went numb. Sally told us later that her first thought was, *Oh my God, what about Raymond and Emily?*

In all our lives we hadn't had any contact with anyone who had cancer, except for Jenny's cousin's wife who died of breast cancer aged about 25. All the way back to Woolwich, Jenny and Sally talked about the shopping and the much worse prospect of how Jenny was going to tell me the news.

When they got back to the pub, Sally took Jenny's dad and her other sisters, Mandy and Wendy, upstairs. Jenny had asked her to tell them but not the kids, as she wanted to tell them with me. We always closed the pub for a few hours in the afternoon on New Year's Eve, to get it ready for the evening, so now we stood in an empty bar.

Jenny was ready to reel off this speech she had worked out in her head about how we would fight it together, and how she would need me to be strong for the kids, no matter what. Her plan was only then to allow herself to let go of the tears that had been trying to fight their way through ever since she heard the news. As she turned to tell me, I'd already sensed something was wrong.

'Alright?' I said.

'No.'

'What do you mean, no?'

'I mean no, I'm not alright.'

107

And that was it, I broke down in tears. Jenny thought we couldn't both be blubbering wrecks, so she didn't cry.

Most of what happened next is a blur in my mind. I didn't take anything in at all. I was in shock. All I could think was that Jenny had cancer. *My Jenny* had cancer. And cancer kills people. You hear about cancer but it's one of those things you don't expect to happen to you. Or at least that was my view. It was so hard for me to understand, I hadn't been through anything like that before, so I had no idea how much chance there was of Jenny recovering. In my mind that day it was cancer equals death. End of story.

I went to pieces. I don't remember feeling like that at any other time in my life – not at the worst moments of my own illness, never. It felt like the world was falling apart and I couldn't do anything to stop it. I was absolutely terrified. The thought of losing Jenny was something I couldn't handle. I couldn't get my head round what it would do to me. I was reeling.

Even now I find it hard to talk about that day. Simply mentioning it gets the tears going and trying to describe how I felt at that moment is incredibly hard. My entire life is built around Jenny and the thought of her being taken away from me was more than I could take, which is why memories of that day still upset me so much.

It was five years after she first told a doctor about the lump. *Five years*. What might have happened if it had been missed again? I can't even think about that.

Jenny told me she was going in on January 7 for the operation to have the tumour – that was its name now, not just 'lump' anymore – removed. I wanted to phone our boss at the company which owned the pub, and tell him to get someone else down to run the pub, but she said, 'No way.'

THE WORST OF TIMES

We had put a lot of effort into that New Year's Eve, our friends and family were coming, so she wanted to make sure we had the best evening possible. I calmed down after a few large brandies and we went upstairs to face my family. They were all trying to hold it together in front of Raymond and Emily, who knew something was wrong but didn't get a straight answer that day.

As Jenny got herself ready for the night she found her lowest-cut top, best push-up bra and shortest skirt and put them on. She wanted to feel like a whole woman and, while a little tumour might change all that in a few days when the operation came around, she was determined not to let it happen that day. She looked amazing, and she was more precious to me than ever before.

Our friends and family arrived. We told a few close friends. Jenny's very good friend Alex was also in the hospital's care, for a tumour on her pituitary gland. Her fiancé at the time, Bob, is a close friend of mine and, like me, quite an emotional bloke. At one point in the evening Bob and me were in the backroom crying together, when Alex and Jenny decided they were not going to let cancer get the better of them or their families. They had a few vodkas and told us to pull ourselves together, it was all going to be fine. Jenny would have the tumour removed from her breast and Alex would have the tumour removed from her head. With their slightly drunk, illogical sense of humour they announced that it wouldn't matter that, after the operations, Jenny would have no boobs and Alex would have no brain. What was all the fuss about?

It was Jenny's way of trying to cope by joking and being strong. I understood that, but Bob and me didn't see the funny side of it. So they left us to it and went for more vodka.

The next day, however, was a very different story. We sat Raymond and Emily down and explained, as best we could, that Jenny had cancer and would be going into hospital for a couple of days, so that they could take the tumour away and make her better. We explained that she would be very sore afterwards as she would be having radiotherapy.

Raymond asked if Jenny was going to die. Holding back the tears, she said no, she wasn't going to die and the doctors would do their very best for her. Raymond went to his room and stayed there for a long time. Emily sat there quietly, and then asked what they had to do to Jenny's boob. She told her they would take some of it away, but she would still have the rest of it. Emily sat for a bit longer and then said, 'Mum, your boobs are so small anyway that when they make them smaller you can have my old bras that don't fit me anymore.'

Jenny and I laughed and cried all at the same time. Jenny says that from that moment she knew she was going to fight it all the way. She was not going to let the cancer win.

On January 2 she went with her friend, Tracy, to the hospital for a bone scan and they told her the cancer had not spread to her bones. What a relief! She was then sent for a mammogram on the same day Emily was at the hospital for an echocardiogram on her faulty heart valve. I joked with them that I was never taking them out together again, as whenever I did they both got their boobs out, which lightened the mood.

After the operation the nurse told Jenny the diagnosis: they had found three cancerous tumours in her left breast and the cancer had spread to the lymph nodes in her left armpit, which meant she would need six months of chemotherapy as well as six weeks of radiotherapy. Jenny told me the only thing she could think of was her hair. The

Happy days – playing well!

Middle left: I swear the water was higher before I got in! Little Raymond, Emily and me, back in our garden paddling pool.

Above: Jenny and me with our grown-up children – Raymond and Emily – at her sister Mandy's wedding to George 'the Puppy' Noble, in August 2005.

Left: On our first holiday abroad, in Cyprus.

Top left: The lovely people of Holland.

Above: In action in Holland.

Left and below: The happy Viking, doing the Viking shuffle.

Left: With Jocky Wilson, one of my personal heroes.

Below: With women's darts legend and good friend Trina Gulliver.

Left: With my family (left to right): sisters Tracy and Julie; Mum and Dad; Jenny, brother-in-law Roy and brother John.

Below: Me and my good mate Rocky. (Andy Jenkins to most people, or 'Jenks'.)

There's no getting away from it – the man is a legend! (Oh, and I'm with Phil 'The Power' Taylor in the bottom two . . .)

Happy times: Our wedding day (left); Jenny's hair starts to grow back in her fight against cancer (below).

Left: Two very important people in my life – Jenny and Peter Stanlick. Sadly, Peter has now passed on.

Three great battles: It took years to win the BDO World Championship title (top), but I lost the title in 2005, the following year (below left). The greatest battle of all has been the fight to save my life, when I shed nearly half my bodyweight (below right).

nurse told her not to be so vain, but, as she rightly pointed out, no one would be able to see the cancer but everyone would see her bald head.

Jenny cried when she told me the news, and that started me off. She was upset and sore from the tests, so everyone was running around for her – not at all what she was used to! She suffered it at first, but soon decided she had to get back to some sort of normality.

I didn't want to go and play in the World Championships a few days later, but Jenny wanted me to. She told me I was a darts player by profession and so I had to go to work. But I couldn't concentrate on my game and got beaten in the first round. I was a wreck, and I couldn't throw a dart to save my life. But the upside for Jenny was that I helped out much more than usual in the pub and with the kids!

Jenny started her chemo in February. The oncology specialists, all the doctors and nurses, were unbelievably brilliant and took time to explain everything to us. They knew how scary the whole thing could be, not only for the patient but for their families as well, and they were there for all of us whenever we needed them. I can't ever express enough gratitude to them.

Once she knew the treatment was going ahead, Jenny's main concern was her hair. It was quite thick and long, and the last time she'd had it short was when she was eight years old. Her doctor, Bruce Bryant, said that her nails might become brittle and her hair would probably thin, which she wasn't looking forward to.

Jenny had to stay in hospital the first time she had chemo, as they wanted to see how she reacted to it. The treatment made her quite sick and, worst of all, she went off chocolate – her favourite food. I tried to do as much as I could, running the day-to-day stuff in the pub, doing the banking, the ordering, even cleaning the beer pipes (which is a very boring job). I think Jenny was pleasantly surprised at how productive I was!

As the weeks of treatment went on, Jenny's hair started to fall out. She was devastated. The staff even banned her from coming behind the bar, because when she turned around a flow of hair would fall out and follow her. As it got thinner, we gradually cut it shorter and shorter, and then the middle started to go. For a while she had a comb-over, and then a hat when she was left with just a very thin layer of hair in the middle, her hairline and fringe.

One day, Jenny's five-year-old nephew asked why she had the same hair as Granddad. She turned to me and said, 'You've got to shave my head.'

'What do you mean, shave your head?'

'I want to shave it all off.'

So we went down to the kitchen and did it. On the outside I was laughing and joking, but, on the inside, having to do that to Jenny was so painful. She could tell I was fighting back tears as I did it, because her cancer was suddenly very real. Before that day I could look at her and almost pretend there was nothing wrong, that she didn't have this terrible illness. But not anymore.

When I'd finished, Jenny looked in the mirror and said she looked like a coconut, which made me smile. Our friend Lorrie, who'd been playing darts in the pub, took over and shaved Jenny's head clean. She said it was a very strange feeling, having skin where you've had hair all your life, and she could now sympathise with men who made a fuss about going bald. 'Don't ever let anyone say it's only hair, because it's a part of you,' as Jenny put it. I offered to shave my head so that Jenny wouldn't be alone, but she said one baldy in the family was enough for her, and anyway – she loved my long hair.

At the time I had been thinking about packing up darts, but Jenny persuaded me not to. She didn't want me to stop and my mate Stevo said I should carry on, if only for the money. I was going out in the first round every time I played, because with Jenny ill I didn't give a shit about darts. But we needed the money so I carried on. It was a bit of a release too, to be honest. I know that sounds selfish, but it's the truth.

While Jenny was having her treatment and I went away for a tournament, she bought all these different wigs. There was one which was exactly like her own hair. When I got back from the tournament and went into the pub, we were all talking away but after 10 or 15 minutes I went quiet. Jenny asked me what the matter was, and I told her I'd completely forgotten about the cancer because she had her long hair back again – or at least what looked like her hair. When I remembered it wasn't hers after all I went to pieces again.

By then, we were trying to carry on with our lives as well as we could. Emily was 11 and in her last year of primary school, Raymond was 12 and in his first year of secondary school. They were doing their best to cope with the situation but it was very hard for them. Jenny was running the pub as best she could, while looking like E.T. (her description, not mine!), and I was away playing darts as usual.

Raymond started fighting in the playground a lot. One particular dinner lady used to come in and tell us about what was happening, which was that every break-time some kids would come along and taunt him, 'Your mum's bald and she's

113

going to die!' Obviously this upset him, and so Raymond would beat the kids up. The dinner lady, who knew what had happened, would let him do it for a while and then tell him to stop. Then he'd say sorry to her. He keeps a lot inside, but when he blows up, well, take cover. Jenny thinks he's a lot like me in that way.

All Emily wanted to know was whether or not Jenny was going to die. Seeing the effect of the cancer on the children was something I'll never, ever forget. Watching them suffer, and seeing how scared they were, was awful. For a while, Emily had this idea that everyone around her was dying. One of her school friends got cystic fibrosis; another one was killed in a car crash while on holiday in Spain; another got a brain tumour and nearly died, and then there was her mum with cancer. It was a lot for a little girl to take all at once.

Emily has a bad heart too. We found out when Jenny took her to the clinic for a routine check-up when she was three. I remember Emily had on a little white dress that day. It's funny, the details your brain keeps hold of. The doctor doing the scan said, 'Oh, we see the murmur is still there.'

'What murmur?' Jenny said, because this was the first we'd heard of it.

'The one she was born with.'

They'd decided not to tell us because, apparently, some parents can't handle hearing it about their newborn kids. Jenny was furious, because her sister has a heart murmur and her mum had heart problems too, so we should have been told. The doctors had known since they did a scan before Emily was even born, and didn't tell us. It's the kind of thing a parent should always be told, even if you don't have the same family history as Jenny.

In the end, it turned out she had a faulty valve in her heart.

In the left side there are three which pump the blood out; Emily has two which pump the blood out and one which pops and drips blood back into her heart. If her heart beats too quickly – if she gets overexcited or too upset – then it leaks faster back into her heart and she could drown in it.

Then they told us that at some point in her life they would have to replace it. If it didn't get any worse as she was getting older, it was best to wait until she was fully grown. From that point she would have to go in for scans every six months, to check how her heart was doing.

After being told about the murmur, we were about to leave when they asked if we had any questions. We said no, but as we were leaving the doctor said, 'One more thing – dental treatment.' He told us she would have to have antibiotics before and after every dental treatment, because there is apparently a germ which grows in your gums, which, if you have Emily's condition and it settles on that valve, can kill you in 24 hours.

When we got home Emily ran off, when all we wanted to do was get hold of her and giver her a cuddle. Jenny and I were both in tears after that. We had a meeting with a doctor at school to tell them how she couldn't get upset and couldn't do PE either. (She didn't actually mind that.)

She still hasn't had to have the operation. When she was 12, in 2001, she did have the valve enlarged. I wasn't much use there either. Emily was being taken down to the pre-operation ward; Jenny and I were supposed to go with her, but at first I couldn't bring myself to. Jenny had to talk me into it.

Then, when it came to kissing her goodbye before the operation, Jenny was fine but I burst out crying. I had to use one of the sterilised towels to blow my nose. I was in such a state that, if Jenny hadn't been keeping an eye on me, I'd have put it right back where I found it. (Not great for hospital hygiene!) As you can tell, I'm not very good at coping with these things. Luckily though, Emily has been fine since then.

While Jenny's cancer treatment was going on, I was picked to play for the England squad at Lakeside in the Six Nations Cup. Jenny came along, as she needed a break and wanted to say thank you to all the people in darts who had sent so many get-well wishes. It was the end of March 1999, and we went with my mum and dad, Jenny's sister Wendy and her fiancé Steve.

We arrived on the Friday; England won, which was great, and everyone was so nice, but on the Sunday Jenny felt unwell when we got home and went up to bed. She stayed in bed most of the time until Wednesday, when she had to organise a birthday party for one of our customers. It was a strain. She went to the GP, who said she'd possibly picked up chicken pox or another virus as her immune system was very weak because of the chemo. I was due to fly to Holland on the Friday but she had to ask me not to go, as she didn't feel she could cope with the pub and kids.

All Jenny wanted to do was sleep. I'd never seen her like that. When I went into the bedroom to see how she was, her face was grey. She had a fever. I took her straight to the hospital, where Dr Bryant shouted at her for not coming in sooner. It turned out that she had septicaemia, and she was admitted for 10 days. Jenny was lying in bed feeling awful, but she said she felt sorry for me because I had to sort out the kids and the pub, and then get moaned at by her if I wasn't at her bedside by 11am to spend the day with her!

Watching Jenny get upset, when I had to go, upset me too.

I desperately didn't want to leave her but had no choice – I had to look after the kids and keep the pub running.

After Jenny had been there just over a week, the nurses said she could go and have a shower instead of the wash-downs she'd had in her room until then. She asked me to get her some new pyjamas so I brought them the next day. The nurse took Jenny to the shower room and told her not to lock the door while she waited outside, just in case anything happened. She turned on the shower and then caught a glimpse of herself standing there bald and naked, weighing about seven stone and holding the striped pyjamas which I'd just given her. All she could do was sit down and cry. The nurse came in to see what was wrong, and Jenny told her she looked like she'd been in a prison camp. The nurse smiled and said she shouldn't look in the mirror.

Jenny was in a terrible state when she came out of the bathroom. I did my best to cheer her up but it was impossible. That was a horrible and distressing time, but it came and went. Life carried on. My darts picked up and the kids started to settle down at school. Jenny started her radiotherapy, which was obviously a drag, although as it was at St Thomas' Hospital during the summer holidays the kids got a few days out in London. We had fun, and one day we even had the police shout, '180!' at us over their loudhailer when they saw me – which embarrassed me but made Jenny, Raymond and Emily laugh. Another time we were going to go on the London Eye, but the queue was too long so we went to the London Aquarium next door instead. That was fun, too.

Days out in London did make it a bit easier to handle for the kids – *Starlight Express*, for example, was brilliant – as it turned Jenny's visits to hospital into a treat every now and then, made it not quite so scary for them. The treatment started in January 1999 and Jenny had six months of chemotherapy, a week off and then six weeks of radiotherapy at St Thomas', right up until the end of September.

I carried on playing darts while Jenny had her treatment. But I wasn't concentrating on my game. Jenny thinks this was when I started drinking really heavily. I already drank more than most but, looking back, it was then that I started drinking at every opportunity there was. If we were going to the hospital for a check-up I would have a couple first to calm myself down, just in case it was bad news. If it was good news, I would be celebrating early. If I had to go and meet anyone for whatever reason, I would drink first to steady my nerves. I started to think I needed it to cope with everything.

One day during her treatment, Jenny woke up unable to move her arm from the shoulder down. She could just about move her fingers so we went to the GP, who sent her for a bone scan, which meant having radioactive dye injected in her arm and then drinking about a litre of water beforehand. Afterwards, we sat in the hospital reception area and hardly said a word to one another. We knew how serious it would be if the cancer had got into Jenny's bones. If that happened, there would be no recovery. The doctors would have been able to keep her comfortable with painkillers until the end, and that would have been it.

We must both have been reading the outpatients clinic board at exactly the same time, because we said in perfect unison, 'That's him, that's the doctor!' This was the doctor – who was *not* Dr Bryant, I want to make clear – who had told Jenny the lump was just a breast mouse, nothing serious, all those years back. He was holding a general surgery clinic right there at the same time as we were waiting to hear if the cancer had spread to her bones.

I was furious. I wanted to go and tell him what I thought of him, but Jenny stopped me by saying it wouldn't do either of us any good for me to be arrested for attacking a doctor. This was at about 10am. All I wanted after that was for the pubs to open, so I could have a drink to calm myself down.

When we went in the radiographer said the scan itself would take about 20 minutes, but that Jenny should go to her GP in two weeks for the results. I saw the look on her face and said I was going for a walk while she had it done. I wasn't allowed in the room anyway.

Poor Jenny lay there thinking, *I can't wait two weeks. What if my arm is like this because it's got into my bones?* She did not want to die. She did not want to break my promise to Raymond and Emily. And then there was her dad – how could she tell him she was going to die before him?

All these things were going through her head when she heard Dr Bryant and me outside the room. I had gone to Dr Bryant's clinic and told him we couldn't wait two weeks to hear whether or not Jenny would die. I couldn't stand the thought of that. After our chat, he went into the consultation room, looked at the scan, spoke to the radiographer then came back out to me.

Dr Bryant told us to go for a walk for two hours and then to go back to his clinic. He would have the results for us. We walked along the high street to the first pub we saw and sat for two hours, just talking rubbish to each other and not really saying anything at all. I couldn't drink fast enough and must have had at least 12 bottles of Pils in that time, but they didn't affect me at all. Jenny was only drinking water, as alcohol now made her feel sick. Eventually, we walked slowly back to the hospital. She made me eat loads of mints before we went back in to see the doctor.

We got to the clinic, sat down and waited for what seemed like ages. Dr Bryant poked his head out of the door, smiled and said, 'Come on in, you.' Suddenly neither of us was worried any more, as he was too jolly for it to be bad news.

Dr Bryant said there was no sign of anything nasty in the scan, and that it must just have been a trapped nerve. He gave Jenny a card to go for physiotherapy and told us not to worry, as she was doing fine. The relief was overwhelming.

I coped in the only way I knew how. We had to go to the pub before we went home, as I needed to sit and have a drink to calm down. When we got back to the pub it was drinks all round, as I was celebrating Jenny being alive.

Jenny Fordham

I have been clear for over 10 years now. It was a great strain on all our lives, but we came through and cancer made me a stronger person. I don't dwell on the bad things in life now; I appreciate my life, and my family, and everyone around me. I don't even have a problem telling people my age, as every birthday is a special one.

Andy, on the other hand – although he realised how precious life and family are – put a lot more effort into his darts and exhibitions. He played all the time and won quite a few competitions. He earned good money and we were living the good life. But along with the work, the competitions and TV appearances came the drinking. He had to drink before a competition, before an exhibition, an appearance or even a radio interview over the phone. If we were going out anywhere he would be ready before me, so he could go down to the bar just for one or two to calm his nerves. He did it before flying, or basically before anything; if we were going out for the day, or with anyone else, even just shopping, he would always find a reason to go to a pub.

SEVEN

BACK UP THE LADDER

Jenny and I got engaged way back in 1980, but didn't get round to taking the next step for another 20 years. Being married or not was never something that bothered us. We lived together, we had kids together, we couldn't have been any more together. To us, marriage was, as the old cliché says, just a bit of paper. So we never bothered with it. Whenever we thought about doing it, something more important would come up.

All that changed after Jenny's cancer. If Jenny hadn't survived, it was possible Raymond and Emily would have been taken away from me because I might not have automatically been their legal guardian, having a different surname. (Jenny was still living under her maiden name of Vallely back then.) The rules aren't clear-cut and we were worried about what would happen if the cancer came back.

I suppose that, if that had been the only reason we wanted to get married, we'd have gone to a registry office and done it any old day. But after all we'd been through, getting married felt like the right thing to do – not just for me and Jenny and what we had between us, but for all our friends and family, the people who'd been with us through those terrible times. We wanted to celebrate the fact that Jenny was alive and we were still together. What better way could there be than to get married?

So we had a huge wedding, but, before any of that, I had to have my stag weekend.

I decided I wanted to go to Scotland for the weekend, so 11 of us went up by train on a Virgin group ticket – calling ourselves the 'Virgin Groupies'. We met at Euston and had a few beers before getting on the train. Just after the train pulled out, two of the lads, Jas and Dal, went to the buffet car to get the drinks in. At the next stop an announcement came over the loudspeaker saying the bar in the buffet car needed to be refilled, because all the beers had already been sold.

After a lot of beers we made it to Scotland and headed to the Swallow Hotel. We left our bags in our rooms and headed for the bar. It was a quiet night to start the weekend. The next day we started with a little pub crawl, but we were missing someone – George Noble, or 'the Puppy' as he's known. I'd known George for years because he was the youngest darts referee in the game when he started out, which was how he picked up his nickname. As I've also already said, he can't hold his drink very well, so he was suffering with a hangover on the morning of the second day and arranged to meet us at the first pub, the Clachan, a bit later. I already knew the owners, Alec and Linda, who were good friends of mine, so it was nice to see them again. We had a few in there and then moved on to the Grapes, up the road. But there was still no sign of the Puppy.

I phoned him to see what was going on and he said he was on his way. When he arrived he said he felt a little bit rough from the night before and needed something to eat, or else he would be sick. Across from the Grapes was a café and a few of the lads, including the Puppy, went over there to eat. As usual, I avoided food and stayed with the beer. About 40 minutes later they started reappearing in the pub in quite a hurry. I asked what the matter was: the Puppy had eaten his breakfast and then asked for a pint of milk, which he downed in one. After a few seconds he brought everything up all over the table – the Puppy strikes again!

Later that day we met up with 'the Goalie', Andy Goram, the ex-Rangers and Scotland goalkeeper who was going to be my best man. My memories of the rest of the day are a bit hazy – days with Goram tend to be like that – but I believe we ended up in a bar called Crofts where we were playing some kind of domino game, which I'm pretty sure Andy made up to get people pissed. No one knew the rules because there weren't any, which meant that everyone lost a lot and had to drink a lot. It worked – particularly on me.

Other people were affected too. At some point in the evening Jas must have fallen asleep, because at the end of the night he was covered in lipstick. I don't remember getting back to the hotel; my next memory is getting up in the night to go to the toilet and hearing snoring coming from the floor at the end of my bed. I had no idea who it was and I even tiptoed over them so as not to wake them up. Once I was in the bathroom I realised the shower curtain had been ripped down for that person to use as a blanket. To be honest, I was so drunk I didn't really care who it was. I went back to sleep and in the morning he was gone. (I found out later it was actually Jas, but why he was there I don't know.)

On the third day, Saturday, we were going to watch the mighty Glasgow Rangers play and decided to start off by meeting in the bar of the hotel. Some old mates came along and we were going to have a few beers and then head off to Ibrox. Unfortunately there were too many of us to get seats all together, but Rangers won so it was happy days anyway. I don't remember the rest of the day very well, but I do have memories of being at a wedding (not mine!) and some people not being too happy about it. One of my mates was going to get bashed so we left quickly. The rest of the night is a blank, which is quite sad really. I hope that means it was a good one.

Sunday was going-home day, but first I'd arranged a tour of Ibrox and, with the help of Jim Duncan, who ran the East Renfrewshire county darts team and used to arrange my exhibitions in Scotland, and old George who worked there, we saw the whole stadium, including the pitch and the trophy room – a dream come true for me. After that, it was time to leave. We got taxis to a bar next to the station and naturally had a few beers while we were waiting for the train. I'm not sure exactly why (it must have been the beer), but I then decided to stay for another night. This was a problem for a few people because they wanted to join me but needed to ask permission from their wives, while others didn't give a shit and could do what they wanted. After a bit of grovelling, most who wanted to stay were allowed to. Although one of them – as I'll explain shortly – played it all wrong.

So now there were a few of us left, we made our way back to the hotel. That night involved having a good drink again and, later on, Peter, Nicky, Jas, Dal, the Puppy and I went for something to eat. After that we wanted to go on somewhere for another drink, but it was late so we didn't know where would be good for us. We got in this black cab and got talking to the driver, who asked if we were up for a bit of fun. We said yes, of course we were, and suddenly the cab lit up like the lights at Blackpool, the music went right up and we set off steaming down the road like a drunken sailor, lurching from left to right. It might have looked weird but it was as funny as hell.

Next we went to the casino, where we had more beer and tried to get rid of some of the money we had left. That night I shared a room with the Puppy, who woke up in the morning and decided to finally tell Mandy (his partner and Jenny's sister) that he hadn't gone home. At the time we were living at The Queen's Arms in Woolwich and Mandy was staying there while we were all away, so she wouldn't have known that he hadn't come home.

The Puppy phoned up and started telling her how we missed the train and had to stay another night. I was on the other bed in the room, trying to make signs to him not to say it, but it was too late. When he got off the phone I told him that another of our mates, Lee, who had got the train back the night before, was working at The Queen's Arms that morning. So if he'd managed to get the train Mandy would know we could have done it too.

About five minutes later Lee must have turned up for work, because the phone went and Mandy was screaming blue murder. The Puppy had done it again. It was a very funny way to end a truly brilliant weekend – even if I don't remember all of it.

* * *

Jenny and I got married on May 27 2000 at Charlton House in southeast London, and we did it properly. We had 150 people at the ceremony and another 170 joined them for the reception. It was huge, and we had the most amazingly special day. Emily was Jenny's bridesmaid, while her maid of honour was her friend Alex, who had been ill at the same time with a pituitary problem which didn't turn out to be serious, thankfully. They all looked beautiful. Jenny pulled a clever one by telling all the guests the marriage ceremony was at 3pm when really it started half an hour later, because she wanted to make sure no one was late!

Raymond was an usher and my best man was Andy Goram, which meant the reception was a riot. He gave a great speech which included a typical Goram joke. He started off talking about how Jenny was a heavy smoker before she got cancer: 'She smoked so much she liked a fag before, during and after sex. Unfortunately for her, she only ever needed one fag!'

Cheers, Andy.

I got my own back on him when we were on holiday in Portugal a few weeks later. Jenny and I had gone with the kids to Lanzarote for two weeks for our honeymoon. We were back home for a week after that, and then went off to Portugal with Andy and a few others. One day, Andy and I went out on a pedalo for a bit of peace and quiet. We headed out to sea for about 10 minutes and then turned back. Suddenly it was really hard work because the tides were totally against us. It took us nearly an hour to get back to shore and, by the time we got there, Andy was totally knackered, dripping with sweat and complaining about his sore knees.

But I was fine. Andy didn't realise that, when he'd been

slaving away, I'd been putting in no effort at all and just moving from side to side as I pretended to pedal, letting him do all the work instead. Revenge was sweet.

Over the next couple of years, the only things that changed about our lives were how much I drank and how big I got. On our first wedding anniversary, in May 2001, we had a barbecue and I drank more in a day than I ever had before and ever have since: 62 bottles of beer before I moved onto about a dozen brandies. That is a frightening amount of alcohol. The strange thing is I remember that day quite well, from seeing everyone to going to the pub and even going to bed that night. I don't know why I was able to take so much, I suppose I was just one of those people who could drink a lot – though my nerves were bad without it. It wasn't a big deal to me. If anything, other people were more proud of it than I was. To me, drinking all that was just something I did, nothing out of the ordinary.

Over the years, the number of people who've wanted to come and challenge me to a drinking competition has been amazing. When it happened, I'd look at them and ask why. They'd say it was because they thought they could drink me under the table, and sometimes that was like a red rag to a bull. I'd say, 'Come on then.' Before long they would be carried out of the pub and I'd carry on having a social drink. I didn't mind doing it to some people, it was quite funny, but it wasn't a good way to behave or a good way to live in the long run. You only need to look at what happened to me over the next few years to know that.

We moved to The Rose in Dartford in October 2003. Being new to the pub, I had to socialise with the regulars and people in the area to get to know them. In one way it was good because we made some really good friends. At the same time my profile as a player was growing (even though I was drinking all that alcohol, my darts was fine), but so was my waistline. I would regularly blame the tumble dryer for shrinking my shirts, but the truth is that Jenny never put them in there. She'd tell me that and I'd reply that the wash must be too hot. The size labels on my clothes gradually moved up, from a 3XL to 5XL, and my weight headed towards its peak of 31 stone, even though I hardly ever ate with Jenny and the kids. I would have breakfast and maybe a sandwich for lunch, and then at about five in the afternoon, when Jenny cooked for herself and the kids, I would tell her to put it in the microwave or that I'd get something later. That happened most days and I'd usually have either a Chinese or a kebab late at night, always after 11pm. Add that to how much I was drinking and it's no wonder I put on all that weight.

My darts was going along quite well in those years, but I wasn't making much of an impact in the biggest tournament of them all, the World Championships. In 2000 I was knocked out by Chris Mason in the quarter-finals; in 2001 I got to the semi-final but lost to Ted Hankey; John Walton put me out in the first round in 2002 and I only made the second round in 2003, when Gary Anderson ended things for me. By then, I'd played nine World Championships and the furthest I'd got was the semi-final. I'd been that far four times, so I was beginning to think that was as far as I would ever go.

But then came 2004 and everything changed.

I always laugh at Jenny when she sees magpies around and thinks they mean good or bad luck. She starts singing the nursery rhyme which goes, 'One for sorrow, two for joy,' and so on. On the first morning of the 2004 World Championship she looked out of our window at the Lakeside and saw two magpies. She says at that moment she knew it was going to be my week. But I didn't see it that way. I had five darts matches to win before I was going to celebrate.

I played Brian Derbyshire in the first round, Tony West in the second and got past both of them quite easily. In the quarter final, I was up against Daryl Fitton. Over the years I'd become good mates with Daryl, and that meant our match in 2004 was one of those really difficult games you get in darts. When you end up drawn against a good mate you really want to win like you always do, but it's difficult to be ruthless against someone you like and care about because you don't want them to lose. That was one of the hardest games I've ever played, and it reminded me of my very first game in the World Championship in 1995, against Nicky Turner.

Daryl and me both struggled to break clear and in the end the game couldn't have been closer. I won five sets to four, even though my three-dart average was fractionally lower than his at 93.57 compared to 93.84. That put me through to yet another semi-final and this time I was up against Raymond Barneveld, the best player in the world, who had just racked up an average of 103.80 by beating John Walton in his quarter-final.

No matter what kind of job you do, there are always going to be certain people you get on with and certain people you don't. Darts is no different. Personally, I try my best to get on with everyone, and I usually do, but there are always exceptions. My main exception is Ray Barneveld.

The bad feeling between us had started before our semi-final, but it wasn't helped by what happened the day before we played. SBS6, the Dutch television company, are one of his sponsors, and when we both got through to the semi-final it meant we were playing at 6pm on the Saturday, the later slot of the two semis. Someone from the BDO came up to me and said SBS6 had asked if they could change the matches around and have Barneveld and me playing in the early game instead, because it was better for the Dutch TV audience back home. The BDO said it was up to me, so I said I'd rather leave it as it was. I knew – and I think the BDO knew too – that the more drink I had inside me, the better I'd play, so of course I wouldn't want to change the time of the match.

SBS6 did interviews with us the day before. They did Barneveld at about 6pm and then me at about midnight. I remember saying something to Arjen van der Giessen, the bloke who did their interviews, about how Barneveld was getting worried because I'd been playing well and was getting closer to him. I was half joking, but Arjen was a bit sheepish and I realised that Barneveld too must have said something along those lines. When the cameras went off I asked Arjen and he said it was true. That was exactly what I wanted to hear.

The next morning, Jenny was at it again with the superstitions. There were two magpies outside our window again, but she also bumped into Elaine Croft – the daughter of Ollie Croft, top man in the BDO – in the Lakeside foyer before the darts started. Elaine said she had a good feeling about the game ahead because there had been a butterfly in the press room that morning. Bearing in mind that this was January, it was very unusual. Elaine said she thought it was her mum, Lorna, who'd sadly passed away but had come back to support me because we'd always got on so well.

I'm not sure I believe in that kind of thing, but it was a nice thought. Jenny's confidence and positive attitude helped me too. Everyone from the pub came to watch, along with Jenny's dad, my mum, Raymond and Emily, and my mate Alf from the pub was there in some kind of jester's outfit.

They were all there cheering me on along with the 1500 other people in the crowd, who made a huge noise when I walked out onto the stage, the biggest roar of support I'd had. The 'Viking' hype had built up through the week and peaked when I came up against Barneveld, because there were Viking hats all over the place. His theme song, 'Eye of the Tiger', probably helped hype them up too.

The commentators said that, judging by our form so far in the tournament, Barneveld and I were closely matched. Everything would come down to which one of us could hit the big shots when we needed to. They also acknowledged how much I'd have loved to get into the final for the first time, just to see if I could win it. The darts commentator Tony Green said I deserved to win before the game had even finished. I don't agree with that. No one *deserves* to win the World Championship title until the moment when they actually do. There's no point saying something like that before it's even happened. He also said that, as the Viking, I'd 'come to plunder'. Very nice, Tony.

We were playing best of nine sets in the semi-final. You played best of five in the first and second rounds, best of seven in the quarter-final, best of nine in the semi and then best of eleven in the final.

I actually started the game well. I took the first leg with a great finish, 120 – it's known as 'Shanghai', after the game of that name where you have to get a treble, double and single to win. The kind of Shanghai I got was a treble 20, then a single and a double to finish. Getting one of those early settled my nerves and I even broke Barneveld in the second leg.

But none of that helped. At the end of the third leg I missed two darts at double 10 to win the leg, and with it the first set and that set Barneveld off. He won three legs in a row and took the first set. The second one went to him quickly too. Barneveld was getting doubles when he needed them and I wasn't. My scoring wasn't bad but I couldn't find the magic when I needed it. I wasn't missing them by much, but that didn't matter. Barneveld was all over me.

Barneveld took the third set, too. We were playing first to five sets and I looked to be in serious trouble. John Walton was interviewed between the third and fourth sets and said that, though the scoreboard might not show it, I had Barneveld worried. My only problem was the doubles. I was creating opportunities by scoring well but not finishing them off.

The second leg of the fourth set ended very strangely. I missed double 10 twice and wasn't looking too clever, but Barneveld actually missed a double one, which very rarely happens to a player as good as him. One of the score sheets – bits of paper on a big pad stuck on the wall – flapped and made a noise when he was about to throw. That obviously annoyed Barneveld and seemed to knock him off his stride. Seeing him get a bit rattled boosted me. I won that set and was then only three-one down.

We had a short break after that. I just sat there with a large brandy and thought to myself, *Oh well, you've reached another semi-final, that's your fifth and that's not bad. You did your best and that was it. A lot of players would be proud of that record.* I didn't really think I'd be able to come back from that far behind against a player as good as Barneveld, one of the best to ever throw a dart.

But even though I was losing, our three-dart averages were virtually identical at around 95.5, which showed that Walton was absolutely right. I knew this and there was a voice at the back of my mind telling me not to give up quite yet.

The atmosphere after the break was incredible. Even Jenny was shouting. She normally never does that because she gets embarrassed, but she and Emily were screaming their heads off right by the stage. They'd moved closer during the break so that they'd be there for me when I lost.

The fifth set got to two legs each and I was throwing first in the decider. It was my big moment, my chance to make it three-two in sets. But I didn't score heavily enough early in the leg and gave Barneveld a chance to get ahead. He didn't take it, so I had a shot at 76 to take the leg and the set. It's a routine finish, treble 20 and double eight, but exactly the kind of shot which had been giving me so much trouble until that moment. Like I say, I'd been creating opportunities to win legs but not taking them because I was missing doubles. Well, suddenly all that changed, because I nailed both shots first time. Now the pressure was on Barneveld and I was the one hitting the big shots.

At the end of the sixth set it went to a decider again, but only after Barneveld had a dart at the end of the fourth leg to go four-two up. He missed it, which left me three darts to get 22. I missed the double 11 and got a single instead, but managed to hit a three and a double four with my next two to take the leg.

At the end of the fifth and deciding leg I had three shots at double nine and missed them all. Not by much, about a centimetre each, but enough to mean Barneveld now had a chance to take the leg and the set. He needed 56. He hit his 20 but landed a single 18 when he needed a double to finish, and then missed his double nine as well. I had another chance from 18. I missed the first one and the second dart was a disaster – I hit a single nine, which meant I couldn't finish as I had nine left. I'd given Barneveld yet another chance, and he took it – which meant I was now four-two down in sets and couldn't afford to slip up again.

If ever there was a moment in my darts career when the pressure was on me more than at any other time, this was it. Everything rested on the next three sets, because if I lost even one of them I'd be out. To be honest, I thought my chance had gone at that moment. I was too far behind and Barneveld only needed one set to win. He wasn't the world number one by accident, and he would have expected to win from that point.

But then something strange happened. Maybe I relaxed a bit because I didn't feel under so much pressure anymore. I don't know. Either way, I started playing some of the best darts of my entire life and at the most important moment of my career. Barneveld might have been way ahead on the scoreboard but he didn't seem dominant out on the stage. The game felt like it was closer than the numbers said and I knew I was playing well.

Then Barneveld starting missing doubles just as I began to hit mine. At the end of the seventh set I went out on a big finish – 93 with a bull, three and double top – and took the set, which made the crowd go wild. I felt good and positive and, most importantly, I was only one set behind. Two to play and I had to win them both.

Between the seventh and eighth sets, Jenny was interviewed

by David Croft from the BBC. She was asked how she was feeling and said, 'I'm calm but I don't know about Andy. His fans are all screaming, his friends are all nervous but I think he'll come back and he'll do it.'

'How can you stay so calm?'

'It's easy. Mind over matter.'

I'm glad one person was feeling calm and confident, and finding it easy. I certainly wasn't!

What helped me was the feeling that most people in the room were supporting me. Barneveld wasn't too bothered by that, because he took the first leg of the eighth set in 11 darts. That was impressive at such a big moment. He followed it up with a 180 at the start of the second leg and I was in trouble. That leg slipped away from me almost as soon as it had started, and suddenly I was staring at defeat. Barneveld had moved up a gear exactly when he needed to, which is what champions do. I was two-nil down in the set, which meant Barneveld needed to win only one of the next three legs and he'd be in the final instead of me. Even worse, he was throwing first in the next leg and so he had the advantage. We both scored heavily, but I hit a double before he did and took the leg. One down, two to go. In the next leg I got ahead early and stayed there. Two down, one to go.

Barneveld was throwing first and hit a 140. I only came back with 60 and it wasn't looking good. But his scores faded and I landed a 180 exactly when I needed to. A few darts later, I had 66 left but Raymond still needed 148 for the leg and the match and it was his throw. He only landed 100 then, so it was my turn to throw the big shots. I went for the bull but only got the outer ring, so it was 25, leaving me 41. Next was an easy nine to leave 32 – a double 16.

One dart, all or nothing. And it landed right bang in the middle. Perfect.

Four sets all, one left to go. Everything to play for. The game was on.

I took the first leg of the deciding set with 13 darts and felt good. I was fired up and enjoying myself. I didn't do much in the second leg and lost it quickly. But I was throwing first in the third leg and so still had an advantage. I opened up with a 140 and didn't look back. I actually felt like I was getting stronger as we got closer to the end of the game, which proved all those people who said my size meant I didn't have the stamina for long matches were talking bollocks. I took that third leg comfortably and now I was one leg away from the final.

Barneveld opened with 100 and I came back with 140. We both got hundreds and then he slipped up with 58 to give me a chance. Another 140 put me ahead. Barneveld only got 59 with his next throws and the window was wide open, because I had at least six darts to get 121 for the match. First was the treble 20 – right in the middle; second, I needed treble 15 and I threw a perfect dart; finally, a double eight ... but I missed it and got a single. No problem, I still had another three darts to score eight.

At this stage my mum, who'd been jumping up and down all evening, was crying. I had a double four to get. My first dart landed just the wrong side of the wire. So did my second. Now I only had one dart left to get me through to the final. And I missed it, landing a single four instead.

My poor mum had her head in her hands!

That left Barneveld needing 90, with all the pressure in the world on his shoulders. He didn't get it. Now I had three darts to get double two for a place in the final and I missed the first one again. But the second one landed right where I wanted it to, and I'd made it. I was through to my first final.

The crowd were standing up and cheering, shouting, 'Andy! Andy! Andy!' It was an amazing moment.

After I won, I turned to Barneveld, shook his hand and said, 'You're probably the best darts player I've ever played against,' because at the time he was. After that he walked off. They started playing 'I'm Too Sexy', I had a little dance to it on stage this time and then went off to see everyone. My mate Ray Stubbs was waiting to do an interview for the BBC; Jenny, Emily and Raymond were waiting there for me.

It was my fifth semi-final and at last I'd got that one step further. When I'd sat there with my brandy during the break I didn't think I'd make it. I thought the semi was maybe the furthest I'd ever go. After four losses at the same stage of the tournament, why should I ever get any further? I'd won plenty of tournaments before, even the World Masters in 1999, but the biggest one of the lot felt like it was slipping out of my reach. So to actually get to the final was brilliant. It was what I'd dreamed of.

Because of the comeback and who I was playing against, it was probably the most memorable match of my life. People still talk more about that game than they do about the final.

To be honest, beating Barneveld in the semi gave me almost as much pleasure as winning the final. We don't see eye to eye and I don't care who knows it. People are always surprised when I say that, but to me it's the same as if I worked in a factory. I work with these blokes and, like in any job, you get on with some of them better than others. That's a fact of life. You can't be best mates with everyone. And Barneveld and me are definitely not best mates.

I found out later what he said after the game: that during the break it was like an alien ship came down, interfered with me and improved my game, whereas he played exactly the same after the break as before.

I'm not a bad loser, but Raymond is one of the worst losers I've ever known. He'll walk offstage, get his bag and go home. He did that after the semi-final, leaving before the final and not showing up for the Champions' Reception like he should have done, as a previous champion. His excuse was that he had a boat booked. I'm sorry, but he had a boat booked to take him back to Holland before the final even happened? What would he have done if he'd beaten me? Still got on that boat and missed the game? I don't think so. I thought that was disrespectful.

On the one hand his aversion to losing is a good thing, as it makes him more successful because he's focused and driven. But there are ways of handling it. He will never turn around and say on the day that the other player was better. You have to play bloody well to beat Barneveld because he's such a great player, so you'd think he would give them some credit. But he never does. He said I must have been helped by an angel when I beat him in the semi-final. I can just about understand him being like that, because he's so desperate to be a winner. But other things have happened which have really upset me.

His wife Sylvia is lovely, and I don't think he realises just how much she does to maintain people's respect. After I won the final there was a bottle of champagne in our room from her, and it wouldn't surprise me if he didn't even know about it. She does that a lot, as other people have noted. I've always got on well with her, she's as good as gold.

In the early days of my darts career, I got on well with

Raymond as well. But he changed the way he was with other players and, for some reason, I became a target. It's a shame, because when I first met him he was a really nice bloke. My view is that the people around him have changed his character. His management seem to have tried to make him more professional, taking him away from the other players; in the past he'd be with the rest of us in the bar, hanging around and having a laugh, but then he stopped.

In 2007, not long after I was ill, I was starting to try to get into the darts again and was playing a tournament at Zuiderduin in Holland. Simply turning up was a big deal for me, because I'd stopped drinking and wasn't very well. To actually go out on the stage and play in front of a lot of people in the venue, and on television, was an even bigger deal. I was in a right state at the time, which meant I played crap. But that was fine. At least I played.

I also knew from the hotel who were hosting the event that all they wanted was for me to show up. They weren't expecting me to play well and had paid me to be there to help sell tickets, so I had a basic fee no matter how well or how badly I played. At the time life wasn't easy and the money was handy for me, so I did it. Virtually everybody there realised how much it meant to me to actually stand up on the stage after everything I'd been through. I had great support, but I was told Barneveld slagged me off in the papers by saying I had an average like a woman. Treating me like that at such a difficult moment in my life showed the kind of person that he is. I don't like him for that.

I've always thought that all Raymond wants is to be liked. He's a brilliant darts player, one of the best I've ever seen, and a very good winner (though obviously not a good loser). I met him for the first time in America in 1994 and he was as good as gold. The first time he got a bit shitty with me was during the Rotterdam Challenge a few years later, which his sponsor was involved in. It was at Rotterdam Football Club and I played him in the semi-final. Most of the crowd were cheering me on instead of him, and I think he got angry because there he was in his home country and the Dutch fans were cheering for an English guy. I beat him, and he stormed off into the players' area backstage and went mad: 'This is my country, they're supposed to be cheering me on, not some foreigner!' and so on.

Richie Burnett and I were out there playing and we both mixed with the crowd, having a laugh and all that, but Raymond kept himself out of the way all the time. My theory is that he was advised badly and someone told him it was a good idea to keep out of the way, as if he was a pop star. I don't see it like that. In my eyes we were lucky to be doing what we were doing, and mixing with the fans was not only part of the job but also part of the fun. I liked being with people, talking and having a drink. I didn't think I was above them. That's who I am and I've always tried to be just me. Raymond seemed to change who he was as he got more successful, and people noticed that. It's sad really, because, as I say, when I first met him he was a lovely bloke.

Barneveld told a Dutch newspaper once that I wasn't a very good player and that I drank too much. What made me laugh was that, soon after, I was asked by the World Trophy tournament organisers to do a photoshoot and some interviews behind a bar for their sponsor, Bavaria Beer, while drinking as much as possible. And who is a part-owner of the World Trophy? Raymond Barneveld. So one day he apparently slags me for drinking too much then the next day his people want me to publicise beer for his tournament? In his book he also has a go at me for making a joke on Dutch TV about how much I drank. Again, for a man sponsored by a beer company to say something like that is very strange.

It's a shame the situation between us has got to this, because I used to get on well with him and our wives are friends. If I was playing him now I'd always shake his hand, but that's it. We're definitely not friends.

But I will always respect him as a darts player. He's one of the best and he's very professional. He has his way of doing things and it obviously works for him. Some people practice at a tournament as soon as they walk in the door – I used to be like that when I was younger. I'd play whenever I could and wherever I could, which was partly to do with how enthusiastic I was – I wanted to throw darts at every possible opportunity. But as I got older and started playing exhibitions I slowed down a bit. You see some players who keep going at the same level and intensity of practice all the way through their careers, putting the hours in year after year, but that wasn't me. Once I'd reached a level of ability where I knew I was a match for just about anyone in the world, I concentrated on trying to get the best out of myself whenever I played. In my own way, I was trying to be professional.

I used to see some players on the practice board all the time and they'd talk about how many 180's, nine-darters and 12-darters they'd hit. It was what boosted their confidence before they went out to play properly. For me, it didn't matter what I did in the practice room. I don't knock other people for doing it, but it wasn't for me.

Different players do different things before games. Colin Monk used to go up to a mirror and snarl at himself to get psyched up. He let the TV cameras see him do that once, which amazed me because he looked really stupid. Some players put on odd socks. Some like to talk to people, others like to be left alone.

All I needed was the drink to get me going. I'd throw a few darts 10 minutes before the game to loosen up my arm, but that was it. The booze was more important because it relaxed me and stopped me from being intimidated by anyone. Unfortunately for my health, I was a better darts player when I'd had a few drinks, so as I became more ambitious in the game I could see no reason to slow down on the alcohol.

Ultimately, darts boils down to who can keep their head together. People say you're just throwing darts at a board, but there is major pressure. You've got the crowd, the TV cameras and the heat to contend with. You have to concentrate on every leg and every throw, working out the scores in your mind and keeping focused. Mentally, the game takes it out of you and is not easy at all to cope with. For me, if I started thinking about things too much I lost my rhythm and concentration. The drink helped keep my mind clear.

That pressure is why darts is so good to watch; it's one man – or woman, sorry! – against another, with no one else there to help. Add in the characters and the crowd and you have all kinds of drama and tension. And of course darts players are normal blokes. We're like the guys from your local pub, and I think that's part of why people like it so much. We aren't like footballers who earn fortunes and live in a different world, we're just normal blokes earning our living.

EIGHT

WORLD CHAMPIONSHIP

After I won the World Championship, my life went crazy. I know it's another cliché, but it really would never be the same again. We stayed at the Lakeside on the night of the final and the next morning I had to go and do an interview with the local TV people downstairs. They wanted me to throw a few darts at a board, but that was the last thing I wanted to do by then. I'd had enough of darts for the time being and I felt like shit.

All I wanted was to go home. I tried to phone the pub to tell them we were on our way back but my phone didn't work. I remember thinking how funny it was that I'd won 50 grand the night before and they'd gone and cut my phone off.

We got back to the pub and it was all quiet outside. But I walked in and it was rammed. I'd never seen anything like it. Not only was it full of people I knew but there were about three television crews and dozens and dozens of press too.

I was happy to talk because I was so pleased about winning the World Championship. My dream had come true and I'd achieved something I never thought possible. But it might not have been the best thing for my health, because I felt I'd proved a point to people who'd been having digs at me for my size. They'd said that, because I was so big, I wouldn't be able to last the distance at the Lakeside because of the heat and the intensity, but I did. Later that year they would be proved right at 'The Showdown' with Phil Taylor, but at the time my stamina was okay.

I thought I'd proved I was strong enough at a darts tournament the year before called the Pentathlon, which lasted all day with very little time to break. There were 20 players in it and you played two legs against every player, then a few other games like Shanghai, round the doubles in 42 darts and a few others. You got points for how you did on each one, starting at eleven o'clock in the morning and playing pretty much constantly until about five, except for a 45-minute break. I won that twice, which should have convinced people that I could take it.

The World Championship is an intense tournament, no doubt about it. At the beginning of the week it's not so bad because you get a day off after you play. There are loads of players involved so there's plenty of time when you don't have a game to play. But it gets busy towards the end of the week, with the quarter-final on the Friday, the semi on the Saturday and then the final on the Sunday. That's tough, really draining, because you're always thinking about the game you've got coming up. Each match is bigger than the last with more and more at stake, which winds you up, and then on top of that, because there aren't so many players involved anymore, you're the focus of even more attention from the press. I'd come through all that and won. I couldn't have been happier.

WORLD CHAMPIONSHIP

After I became World Champion (I know I've written that a few times already – but I like seeing it in print so I'm not going to stop!) I couldn't believe the attention I was getting from the media. It didn't stop for days and days, or months in the end.

Now that was a strange feeling. In some ways, I couldn't work out what was going on, why they were so interested in me. It's not really my thing, all that celebrity stuff; at the beginning, when I was just having a laugh, it was all new so I just got on with whatever I was doing and enjoyed myself. But after a while it got a bit too much, especially as I didn't set out to become famous. All I wanted to do was win darts tournaments. Fame was a by-product of that.

I got home on Monday at lunchtime, after I'd done the interview at Lakeside. At about ten that night I looked at Jenny and said, 'I'm fucked. I'm going to bed and I'm not coming down until tomorrow.'

The next day, Tuesday, I didn't come down at all. I more or less stayed in bed all day. Physically, I was absolutely knackered. I couldn't take any more and needed to rest. The woman from the *Daily Mail* got quite upset when Jenny told her I wouldn't be coming down that day, but in the end she wrote that I was a nice bloke and a gentle giant, which was good.

(She did also ask me if I had any skeletons in the cupboard – what a daft question! Even if I did, did she honestly think I'd tell a woman from a newspaper?)

All the fuss started again that day. My phone was ringing all the time. After a while I couldn't take any more, so I gave it to Jenny. She had to look after my phone – which was ringing all the time – her own phone – which was ringing all the time – and the pub phone, which was also ringing all the time. Looking back, I feel quite sorry for what she had to cope with that day!

I didn't have a manager at the time so I didn't have anyone to take care of all that stuff for me. I'd get one soon afterwards, but for those few weeks it was just us and we coped as best we could.

The attention seemed to carry on for ages. We even had people in the pub who just sat there staring at me. A few weeks later this bloke came in every day for a whole week. He barely spoke to anyone, just sat there on his own, which everyone thought was a bit odd. On the Friday I was up early and left the pub before it opened, because I was going off to a tournament. Jenny came downstairs to open up and the guy was there again. He asked if I was about that day and Jenny said, 'No, Andy's away for the weekend.' She thought this bloke was a bit strange so she asked why he was interested. It turned out he had a week off work and decided to come down to the pub and spend it around me. He was hoping to get an autograph before he went home and was really disappointed when he heard I wasn't going to be around that day.

He'd sat there for four days and hardly spoken to me – just a hello here and there – then waited until I'd gone to ask for an autograph. It's quite frightening really, what some people do. Why would a bloke want to sit and look at a 30-stone man like me for a whole week? I never saw him again after that week, and it's probably for the best.

For a long time after that people would appear in The Rose who'd come along especially to meet me. They even came all the way from Holland. It's nice when people do that – come in, say hello, be friendly and ask for a photo. I'd much rather they did that than sit and stare and try to take sneaky pictures.

It's got worse now that I look so different after losing all the weight. People see me and I can hear them talking. One will say, 'That's him, it's the Viking, I'm sure it is,' and then his mate will go, 'No, it's not. That's never Andy Fordham.' Now people stare even more than they did before, but I'm getting used to it. The happier and healthier I get, the easier it is to handle.

I like it when people come up and shake my hand. I was having lunch in a pub in Hammersmith in 2008 and two guys came up to us. At the time I was quite ill and had been in the papers, talking about my recovery. All they wanted to do was shake my hand, wish me all the best and say they hoped I got better. They didn't even want autographs, just to say get well soon.

I'd been a bit low before that and was worried about the future, so it made me smile. Thanks, lads.

The worst is when people are pissed up and grab me round the neck. They don't mean anything by it and are really just being affectionate, but it's happened a few times that a guy has put his arm around my neck and pulled me towards him for a photo. I hate it, I really do!

Back in 2004, before I got ill and it was still all new to me, I enjoyed the attention. After a while I started getting invited to different events and got a manager, which made life easier. I had some brilliant times, some great nights and met the kind of people I never thought I'd ever come close to. I was really lucky with how people treated me too, and made some great friends. I think it's because, with me, what you see is what you get. I've never tried to be anything different to what I am and I make sure I'm nice to people. Most of them are nice back, although, with some celebrities, you meet them and then wish you hadn't. (I won't say who, though!)

The best are Ant and Dec. They're brilliant fun. Bristow and me got them really drunk once. As part of the 'Ant and Dec Challenge' bit of their Saturday night programme, they wanted to play a darts match against each other and they recruited Eric and me to be their coaches.

We met on a Tuesday morning at the City Darts pub (now the Princess Alice), up in Commercial Road. My daughter came with me and I'd been drinking since about 8am, as usual. We got there at about quarter past nine and had to bang on the door to get in. I asked if there was any chance of a drink, and of course there was. We were having a few beers with Eric when Ant and Dec arrived. Bristow took Ant upstairs to one dartboard, leaving me with Dec, who was in a sling.

I wasn't happy about that at all. I hate losing at anything, and with Bristow it's even worse, because not only is he a mate and a bit of a hero to me but he's also competitive too, and loves a bit of banter. So with Dec in a sling, my chances of winning did not look good.

Luckily it wasn't his throwing arm. So we had a couple of throws and I said, 'Look, if we're going to do this properly, you need a beer.'

He went, 'No, don't worry, I'm alright.'

So I told him he didn't have a choice. (This was about half past ten in the morning, by the way.) Dec looked at the camera crew.

'It'll be all right if I have a beer, won't it?'

One of them piped up, 'Well, it's darts so you probably should.'

I didn't even ask him what he wanted. I just went and got him a bottle of Bud. We started practising and, after a while, I told him he couldn't throw with the sling on and had to take it off.

150

'Yes, but . . .'

'I don't care. Take it off.'

So he took it off and I went to get him another bottle of Bud. By now he was getting into the swing of it and we were having a laugh. The next thing, Bristow and Ant came down. Ant saw Dec didn't have his sling and asked where it was.

Dec said, 'Andy told me to take it off.'

Ant looked at me. 'So you're a doctor now, are you?'

They're a great couple of characters. Next, the four of us went upstairs to play a game, Bristow and Ant against me and Dec. I was feeding them drink all the time, which was just something I did. I know it's wrong now, but at the time it was fun. (I didn't need to feed Bristow, mind you. He can look after himself very well without me.)

Me and Dec won that game and then we went downstairs to discuss what we were going to do on the Thursday, when we were due to come back again. We'd been there for about half an hour talking and I think I'd got about three double vodkas down each of them. Ant was by the window, slurring down the phone to his future wife, and Dec was hanging off the bar. Dec had finished with his drink so I took it over to Ant.

'No, no, I don't want that!' he said

His fiancée asked what the matter was.

'Andy's trying to force another vodka down me.'

She must have been telling him not to drink it, but in the end he did. A bit later I said I had to go.

'Why? Where are you going?' they asked together.

'I've got to go and do *The Paul O'Grady Show*.'

'You can't go and do that. Look at the state of you.'

'The state of me? What about you two?'

'Ah, whatever. We're going to the pub!'

So off I went and I didn't see them again until the Thursday, two days later, when we met there again.

Thursday came and I was sitting in a pub across the road from the studios where we were going to do the filming. This woman came in and sat down with me.

'Where are they?' I asked.

'Well,' she said seriously, 'we need to have a chat before you see them.'

'Why is that, then?'

'There can't be any alcohol involved today.'

'Okay, but that's not my fault,' I said. 'They're old enough to say no.'

'Maybe. But when they came to work on Wednesday they could only stay for about 45 minutes before they had to go home. I have never, ever seen them in such a mess.'

It turned out they did go to the pub later and stayed there. That was it, they were done for after that. So on Thursday we met in the pub round the corner from the studios. I had my drink and they pulled up outside. The doors slid open and I banged on the pub window, showing them the drink. We went and watched them do the show and then headed up to the VIP bit afterwards. Everyone was there having a chat when this girl came up to me and said, 'I don't like you.'

I remembered Ant slurring into his phone in the pub while I gave him more vodka. 'You're his fiancée, aren't you?'

'Yes I am.'

She wasn't happy, so I had to apologise. I hope she's forgiven me now. She spoke to Jenny afterwards, but I didn't get an invitation to the wedding.

I've met those two a couple of times since and they are brilliant, two of the nicest, funniest blokes you could ever wish to meet. What you see on TV is exactly what they're like in real life, brilliant fun. I hope to meet them again one day. You never know.

(It's funny how, when you see then on TV, it's always Ant on the left and Dec on the right. Someone told me it's in their contracts that they always have to be that way round. Makes sense, really.)

I suppose I can't finish that story without saying who actually won the darts –well, it wasn't me and Dec. When we were practising I told him to aim down the left of the board rather than going for 20's, because he'd score more that way. There are consistently higher numbers down the left while around the 20 there are numbers like five and one which are of no use.

But when the actual game started it didn't go so well. In fact it wasn't even close. They were playing to see who could get the most points with nine darts and Dec threw first. Ant didn't even need to throw his last three darts to win because he'd already scored more with six than Dec did with nine. It didn't help us that Dec was the one with a bad shoulder. But it was his left arm, so it probably didn't make much difference.

One of the other funny TV shows I did was *Celebrity Darts*. Me and Bobby George were the captains of the two teams. He had Holly Willougby, James Hewitt, Mike Le Vell and Phil Tufnell, while I had Rowland Rivron, Vicky Butler-Henderson (who is a lovely lady), Keith Chegwin and then there was Mr Vegas.

Johnny Vegas is some character. He had the entire pub in fits of laughter just about every time he opened his mouth. Once he starts, he just goes off on one and you can't stop him.

Bobby had his team at his house to practice and I had my lot round to the pub where I lived. Before they arrived, the producer had a word with me about Johnny, telling me not to let him drink too early. But what could I do about it? If he wanted a Guinness, what could I say? She said they were trying to keep him off the booze a bit, so I said I'd do my best.

So in they came one by one, with Vegas last. I said hello to them all and he gave me a big cuddle, as he always does. We'd met briefly once before, when he came to watch the darts, but he was with a few people so he didn't mix much with the players. He's a diamond, Johnny – one of the funniest, most genuine people I've ever met and a total one-off. I've never known anyone make people laugh like he does, it's like he's on a different planet. Once he starts, that's it, you know everyone is going to be pissing themselves.

But he does like a drink. When he came into the pub that morning, the producer even asked if he wanted one. After what she'd said to me I couldn't believe she was offering him alcohol. And sure enough, he wanted a drink.

In his northern accent he went, 'Ooh, I'll have a Guinness.'

Well, that was him off and running. It was about quarter to nine in the morning and we were due to start training at half past ten. Rowland Rivron wasn't well, I think he had food poisoning or something, so my team was down already. We had a little team meeting to discuss everything and I gave them all a set of darts. Then they went to have a little throw and I watched to see if I could give them some tips. There wasn't much I could do to help in the end, but I tried. After that they were left to muck around with the darts on their own for a while.

A few pints later, I heard Johnny shout in triumph, 'Yes! Yes!'

So I went over and asked what the matter was.

'It's my focus,' he said, pretending to throw a dart. 'My focus, it's right there. Right on that treble 20. I'm nailing it every time. I'm there. Right there.'

'Right. How many pints have you had?' I thought I'd ask, so I'd know how many he needed to get him going properly.

'Eight.'

That's a few, but fair play, if that's what works for him. So they carried on throwing and about an hour later, I heard him shout again.

'No! No!'

So I went over and asked what the matter was this time. He looked totally different now, not happy at all.

'It's my focus,' Johnny said. 'It's gone. Completely gone.'

I tried to help because he really did look upset.

'When you look at the dartboard, what can you see?'

And he said something I will never, ever forget. 'All I can see is a box of abandoned kittens.'

'You what?'

'A box of abandoned kittens. And it gets worse.'

'What do you mean, it gets worse?' I asked, almost doubled up laughing by now.

'They're not getting on!'

By then I'd had it. I just cracked up.

Later on they had to do an interview each. When Johnny did his, everyone listened. He started talking fairly normally (for him) about how darts wasn't easy, and then suddenly he broke off in his own unique way.

'There's demons on that Lakeside stage, I'm telling you. It's haunted. There are demons out there waiting for me.'

Everyone lost it. He was lucky the camera was on a tripod which could hold it steady, because the cameraman was all

155

over the place. I had to step away because I didn't want to see myself cracking up on TV. Vegas is such a funny man.

Of the others, Vicky was a lovely lady but Rowland was a bit weird. It might have been because he was ill, but he was an odd one. When they arrived for the competition they had to come in one by one to pretend they were arriving separately. When Chegwin arrived I said, 'You're not going to get naked are you?' I'd seen him do his jungle programme in the nod and really didn't want him throwing darts with everything hanging out.

But he wound me up because, when the producers asked if he was ready to come in, he shouted, 'Yes, I'm naked and ready to go!'

Luckily, he was only joking as he popped his head round the door to laugh at me. He's someone I was wary of at the start. I didn't know what to expect, especially as he's so loud on the telly and people who play up like that away from TV tend to get on my nerves. But Chegwin is such a nice man – kind, genuine and fun to be around. He seemed to be really enjoying himself as well, which I liked, and he never played the big man, never expected any favours because of who he is. (Bear in mind that in TV he's a proper star, he's been around for years.)

One day during filming, he brought some friends along to watch and afterwards they wanted photos taken with some of the team members. Chegwin didn't just walk up and expect people to have their photo taken. Every single person he went up to, he'd wait until they stopped talking and say, 'Sorry to interrupt, but could I ask a favour? Would you mind having your picture taken with my friends and signing this for them?' I thought that was brilliant. He was a different class, Chegwin, I liked him a lot.

Next it was Johnny's turn to arrive for the cameras. I wondered what he had up his sleeve for that moment.

The door opened, he took one step in, looked at me and went, 'Dad!' and gave me a hug. Everyone burst out laughing and his jokes just went on from there, non-stop. We got on well – we both used to like a few drinks – and I went out with him a couple of times after that. He seems to have this natural gift for entertaining people, it doesn't matter where he is or who's around him, he's just hilarious.

We were over in Maidstone at a hotel once and I was waiting for him to do a bit of filming for another programme about smoking. I was with the producer in the car and she phoned him to find out how long he'd be as he hadn't left his room yet. When she hung up, she was laughing. Apparently he was watching *Jeremy Kyle*, and said he wouldn't leave his room until someone gave Kyle a smack in the mouth. It's the way he says things that cracks me up. He wasn't bad at darts either.

Phil Tufnell was something else. When the matches between the teams started he was paralytic. He'd been drinking large vodkas and Red Bull all day and was a mess. He was making a lot of noise and threw his darts in the lake when he still had a game to go. During a break the producers pulled me aside – me, the man known for being one of the biggest drinkers ever in the world of darts – and asked me to slow them down on their drinking because they were worried it would spoil the show. But I couldn't help them, it wasn't up to me. From then on it was chaos – a good laugh, though.

When Vegas played Keith, he was asked about Chegwin for his interview. He started saying how nice Keith was: 'When he says Merry Christmas you can tell he really means it. Not like me. When I say Merry Christmas, what I really mean is I want to shit on your bed.'

I don't know where it comes from. His mind is something else, and he's so quick. If you watch him you can see when he's about to start. Someone will say something and his eyes will start moving from side to side as he thinks, and then – *bang!* – off he goes. After his Chegwin interview they got me up on stage and tried to ask me questions, but I couldn't even talk because I was laughing so much. What a great character.

That night, I was so drunk I gave up at about half past ten. I found out later that Jenny struggled to get Vegas to leave at 1am. He was staying at a hotel near Brand's Hatch. Someone came into the pub the next day and told us that they found him the next morning in reception, asleep on a sofa with his trousers round his ankles. Apparently, when he got back to the hotel there was some kind of convention going on. They spotted him and asked him to come in for a drink – which, Vegas being Vegas, he was more than happy to do. And one drink became a few more.

I spoke to him afterwards and asked if it was true. He said he'd woken up, realised where he was and that his trousers and pants were round his ankles, so he jumped off the sofa and tried to pull them up. Because he did it so quickly they got all tangled up, and he said it looked like he was wearing a nappy. Oh dear.

The only other person who makes me laugh like that is my mate Colin Monk, another darts player. I only have to look at him and I crack up. I have no idea why. The other day he rang me up and said, 'Bonjour, bonjour,' and I just burst out laughing. I guess some people just do that to me.

Another time I went to a celebrity golf day. There were a

few people there playing and I phoned my mate Andy Goram to tell him Matt Le Tissier, another footballer, was playing. Andy said, 'Tell him he's a plonker.'

I'd had a few drinks so I thought it was a good idea. I went up to Le Tissier and said, 'Alright, Matt, how are you doing?'

'Good, thanks Andy. Nice to see you.'

'You too. I've got something to tell you.'

'Oh yeah, what's that?

'My mate thinks you're a plonker.'

Matt stopped smiling. 'What? Who said that?'

'Andy Goram.'

The grin came back again. 'Oh, him! What a wanker.'

They were mates, so he didn't mind. He's a nice bloke, Matt Le Tissier.

Most of the celebrities I met were decent people who seemed to appreciate their success and had good manners, but who also liked a laugh. They were good days.

NINE

THE SHOWDOWN

With my new status as World Champion, the money on offer was much more than it used to be and I wanted to make the most of the opportunities which came my way. A few months later, I went off to Holland, one of my favourite places, to do a few exhibitions. Phil Taylor – the PDC World Champion – happened to be doing one in a pub quite close by as well and one of my mates suggested we go down there to see him after I'd finished. My exhibition was in the afternoon and his was in the evening; you shouldn't really turn up at other people's, but we did it anyway and Phil didn't mind. We were talking about a few different things and then he said, 'How about you and me play some time? Head to head?'

That seemed like a good idea. 'Okay, sure. Why not?'

Phil said he'd sort out the money side of things with Barry Hearn, chairman of the PDC. I said that was fine, but he had to let me tell people my own way. The relationship between the PDC and the BDO hadn't improved over the years, and

I wanted to avoid any problems with the BDO because I was still with them. Phil put his hand out and we shook on it. That was it, the deal was more or less done right there and then. I knew some people from the BDO would try to talk me out of it, so my plan was to get the contract signed and only then tell the BDO. I knew I was going to annoy some people by going ahead with it, but I had to be sensible. How could I say no to 50 grand for a day's work? It was serious money.

When I spoke to someone from the BDO, who I won't name, he started telling me not to do it, exactly as I expected he would. I just said, 'Okay, you go and explain to Jenny why I can't go and earn that 50 grand because I won't be able to look her in the eye and tell her.'

After that, they at least understood my point of view. The BDO didn't want me to play but they could see why I was going to. I told the BDO's PR man, Robert Holmes, first, so he could put the story out in the best way possible for them. I think they appreciated that. I didn't want it presented as anything to do with the rivalry between the PDC and the BDO, because it just wasn't. Darts had had so much publicity that year that there was simply huge interest in seeing me play Phil, which meant there was an opportunity for us to make some decent money. So it was all set up and we were due to play in November.

And then I went and broke my wrist. Rather badly, as it turned out.

I was out in Holland again (I couldn't stay away from the place!), for a tournament in August with Martin Fitzmaurice. We got back to our hotel quite late at night after the darts and a few drinks, and found the front door was shut so we headed round the back. It was raining outside, very finely as I remember, and at the back there was a wooden slope down to the door. Martin went first and told me to be careful not to slip. As I was a big lad he was worried about me.

I'd actually fallen over with Martin as we tried to get into another hotel after a late night in Holland, not long before. It was pouring with rain and I'd landed quite hard. Martin thought I might have hurt myself badly.

'Can you move your arms?' he asked.

'Yes,' I replied.

'What about your legs?'

'Yes, they're fine.'

'Okay, take your time and get up slowly.'

I tried to stand up and fell over again.

'No, go slowly,' Martin said.

I tried again and fell over for a second time.

'No, I said go slowly!'

'I would if you weren't standing on my hair!'

The silly sod hadn't realised he was stopping me getting up. Once he moved it was fine. We got into the hotel with no problems, except for being soaked through.

I hadn't hurt myself that time, so when it came to the slope on the night that I'm telling you about, I wasn't worried and just said, 'Yeah, yeah, I'll be fine.' But I put one foot down and that was it, both feet disappeared from underneath me.

As I fell, I instinctively stuck out my hand under me to cushion my fall. Unfortunately it was my right hand. For some reason which I still can't work out, I made that hand into a fist while I was in the middle of the fall, and when I landed I put all my weight through it onto the hard ground. Bearing in mind that I weighed about 30 stone at the time, it's no surprise that it really fucking hurt.

ANDY FORDHAM - THE VIKING

I went to bed as normal (it might have fucked up my liver in the long run but the drink was a pretty good painkiller in those days) and in the morning Martin knocked on the door of the room I was sharing with Stevo. Those two went off to breakfast and I decided to get a shower first. My hand was really sore but I kept on moving it, because I thought that would be the best thing for the injury. I didn't want my wrist to get stiff because I had to play darts.

I went into the bathroom for my shower and saw my deodorant on the shelf. The floor in the bathroom was tiled and slippery, so I thought, *Make sure you grab that on the way out, so you don't have to come back in here in case you fall over again.* I had my shower, my hand hurting all the time, and then I got out. I went and sat on the bed, looked back into the bathroom and saw my deodorant still in there. *Bollocks, I forgot it!* Then, out of the corner of my eye, I saw a can of Sure poking out of the top of Stevo's bag. *Result,* I thought, *I'll borrow his.*

I struggled on with my underwear and trousers and then got my socks and trainers on. It was really hard work, because my hand was so sore that by the time I'd done up my laces I was hot and sweaty and really not happy. I thought I'd put some deodorant on before I did my shirt, so I grabbed the can and started spraying.

I wanted to stop myself from sweating, so I was having a proper go with the deodorant when I realised something wasn't right. I looked down and there was white stuff everywhere. Like a muppet, I'd grabbed Stevo's shaving foam and was spraying it all over myself. I was standing there swearing my head off when the door opened, and in came Stevo and Martin. They looked at me and looked at the foam everywhere.

'Don't ask,' I said. 'Just don't fucking ask.'

But the sight of me with no shirt and covered in shaving foam made them piss themselves laughing. I was furious, though eventually I calmed down, cleaned myself up and got dressed.

A few days later I went home and then came back to Holland as I was due to play again. By then it had been 17 days since I fell over and I hadn't thrown a single dart because my hand hurt so much. I also hadn't been to the hospital or the doctor.

I was due to play that night and I realised I was going to have to try to throw a dart at some point, so I went to practice that afternoon. My first dart was aimed at the 20. As I threw it, it went down and down all the way into the big 19, nowhere near where I'd wanted it to land. What the hell was going on here? I had a few more throws but they weren't any better. My hand was killing me. I tried to take the pain away by drinking some more, but it didn't work. There was no strength at all in my wrist. It was useless.

All week I kept saying, 'It'll get better, don't worry. I'll be fine.' But on the Friday, one of the drivers from the hotel made me go to hospital. After he'd had a look at me, the doctor said they would do an x-ray and they put me through one of those huge white scanner machines where you lie down on a flat surface and it moves around with you inside it. That was a palaver too. First of all they had to put an extra bit of wood under me to make it strong enough to support my weight. Then, instead of just putting me on my back, I had to roll onto my front and put my right wrist above my head so that I was lying there face down, looking like Superman flying into this great big machine.

Afterwards I was sweating like a pig. After a while the

nurse came back in. All the time I'd been moving my hand backwards and forwards, like I had ever since I fell over, because I didn't want the joint to seize up. It didn't hurt all that much and I thought I was doing the right thing. Anyway, the nurse saw me doing it and said, 'Stop, you can't do that, it must be really painful!'

'Why can't I do it? If it was that painful I wouldn't move it at all.'

'It's broken! Your wrist is broken.'

Oh shit.

The doctor came in straight away and said it was actually worse than just broken. Apparently, because I fell onto my fist, I'd pushed one of the bones in my hand back into my wrist and it had split one of my arm bones down the middle, which made my right arm a little bit shorter than the other one. He said it needed to be pulled back out and pinned in place, but because it had been nearly three weeks since I fell over the bones would have healed slightly and I shouldn't really have it done. Instead, I should just let it mend on its own. My wrist wouldn't be the same again, but anything else would do more harm than good. He told me 12 days was the cut-off point for treating a break like mine and it had been more than 20 since I did it.

I was going back to England the next day, so the doctor advised me to go straight to the hospital in London to see if they could do anything. I did what I was told and the doctors in the UK didn't mess around. They took me in immediately and operated the day after that. I had three pins put in, two in the side and one in the top, to hold the bones in place.

Before I went in for the operation, I remembered all the things I'd heard about what general anaesthetics can do to really big blokes like me. Apparently, big guys suffer badly when they come round and can even die if things go wrong. So when I saw the anaesthetist on the way in, I was a bit nervous.

'Make sure you don't give me too much, won't you?'

He smiled to reassure me. 'Don't worry, I won't give you too much.'

He was trying to help but it only made me panic again. 'But don't give me not enough either!'

I remember him smiling and that was it, I was under.

The next thing I knew I was waking up in the recovery room. I could hear a woman screaming and I remember a nurse standing over me and pushing my arm down. For some reason I was lying there trying to throw darts. I kept trying to bring my arm up again and the nurse kept pushing it down. It was ridiculous!

When I came round properly, the nurse asked me how it felt and, because it hurt, they gave me some more morphine. But it still hurt so they gave me more. In the end I had the maximum dose and was as high as a kite, which felt pretty good as it happens. But after that day, my wrist didn't ever hurt again and I didn't have to take any more morphine.

A few days later Barry Hearn saw me with the plaster cast on my hand and asked me if I was going to be alright to play, because this was August and I was playing Phil in November. The contracts were signed and the deal with Sky TV was being done, so they needed to know. I said I'd be fine and they asked me to get a doctor's note confirming it. I went to the hospital for my normal appointment and asked the doctor for the letter. But he said he couldn't sign because he didn't know for certain.

The doctor wouldn't change his mind and, a couple of

weeks later, I went to have the three pins taken out. They were a few inches long and had hooks on the end where they poked out of my skin. People kept telling me it would be fine and wouldn't hurt at all, but I didn't believe any of them. It was easy for them to be so confident when their arms didn't have pins in!

So in I went. I sat down and stuck out my arm. Luckily, the nurse looking after me was superb. She was talking to me all the way through, trying to keep my mind off what was going on but telling me what the doctor was doing at the same time. She said he was going to grab the end of the pins with these things which looked like pliers and then he'd have to pull and twist to get them out. I was not enjoying myself one bit, I can tell you. I closed my eyes and took a few deep breaths, preparing myself for the first one.

Christ, this was going to hurt!

Then I heard the nurse's voice, 'That's the first one done.'

What? I didn't feel a thing! I thought she was joking. But she wasn't. I looked down and the pin was in a little bowl next to me. They did the other two and, as with the first one, I didn't feel a thing, except on the last one when he caught a few of the hairs on my arm in the pliers. There was a fair bit of blood but it didn't hurt at all. They wrapped me up in a bandage and, two days later, I went to see the physio. He was amazed at how much movement I had in it, which was great news. I think that was because I'd moved it so much in the weeks after I hurt it. I'd been very lucky, really.

The next week I had to go to a press event with Phil Taylor, to publicise the game, and the first thing Barry Hearn said was, 'Thank God you've had that plaster cast taken off!'

To recap: I'd fallen over in the August, had the operation a couple of weeks later and then had the pins taken out six weeks after that, which would have been towards the end of October, not long before we were due to play. Sky had put a lot of money into the match – christening it 'The Showdown' and publicising it everywhere. No wonder Barry was nervous!

I started throwing again, with only a couple of weeks to go before the match, and I was really struggling. I had no strength in my wrist at all. All the power had gone while my hand was in the plaster cast. I tried everything to build up the muscles again. I had one of those squeezy balls and a little thing with a spring on, both designed for hand exercises; I used them all the time as I tried to get it going, but nothing seemed to do much good.

Daryl Fitton came down the day before I played Phil and I was struggling to hit a 20, let alone any good scores. Before that I had been desperate for games. A young lad called Steve Douglas came to the pub once and I needed a game so badly I gave him 50 quid to play me. We played best of 21 legs, so it was first to 11, and he beat me. But at least I got some throwing done.

When Daryl appeared, I was still struggling. That was on the Saturday, and Sunday was game day. My mate Andy Goram was down and, when I found him at about half past ten on Sunday morning, he was already in the pub. We'd had a load of booze the night before and went to bed at about one o'clock, starting again at half past ten in the morning. We were having a few beers, a few white wines and brandies, and playing a bit of pool until about half four in the afternoon, when I went to get ready to play Phil.

By the time we left, I'd probably had about three bottles of wine, four or five beers and about the same number of brandies. Drinking that much is wrong. I can't believe I used to do it, but I didn't even think about it much at the time. I just drank whatever was in front of me. I don't know how I did it, to be honest.

When we got to the venue, I plonked myself down at the bar. Phil was round the corner, practising away as he always does, while I had a few more drinks. We were due to start playing at half past nine and I went off to start practising at about eight o'clock, which meant I'd been drinking for about nine and a half hours before I even had a throw. I have no idea how much I'd had to drink by then.

It was getting nearer and nearer the start and I was doing a few interviews. I was having a chat with Helen Chamberlain when she asked me how my wrist was. 'It's alright, I'll be trying my best, make no bones about it,' I said, making a joke without even realising it.

We were called down to walk on, but I don't remember it; neither do I remember walking out onto the stage, which is a shame because the next day someone spoke about the girl who walked on with me. Apparently she was lovely, and was wearing a see-through dress with a thong on underneath it. I was walking behind her, but I've got no memory of it at all – I'm gutted!

All I remember about the start is the atmosphere, which was absolutely mental. There were a few games before we came on, with Eric Bristow, John Lowe, Wayne Mardle and Roland Scholten playing, and the crowd were going wild during those matches. When I started practising backstage there were cameras on me straight away, and the pictures were shown on the big screens down in the venue. You could hear the roar from the crowd when they saw me. Then the cameras went onto Phil and there was another huge roar.

That was probably the best atmosphere I have ever played

in. It was madness. We both had a lot of support but I probably had a little bit more. That only happened because for one I was very much the underdog and, secondly, because we were playing close to where I'm from. If we'd played in Phil's hometown up north then he'd have had more support than me.

Everyone thought I was going to get smashed by Phil because of my wrist and because he's such a great player, the best ever. But after we'd played four sets it was two each. I was talking to a bloke who works for Sky, and he said one of the best things he heard was darts commentator Sid Waddell shouting at the top of his voice, in that brilliant way he does, 'We've got a game on!'

We had a break before the seventh set and by then Phil was four-two up. I was quite pleased with how I was playing but I was missing a lot of doubles. A few of the sets were going to three-two in legs, so it wasn't a hiding at all. The thing with Phil is that he's so brilliant that you can leave yourself with a straightforward two-dart finish and he'll be on something like 190, quite far behind, but his last dart will leave him on an easy finish which you're 99 per cent certain he'll get. That means the pressure is back on you to finish with those two darts. Obviously it works, because he's won so many times. He's a truly brilliant player, just amazing.

We went for the break after six sets, and in that time you can have a cigarette, a Coke, whatever. Obviously I had a bottle of Pils and a brandy waiting for me. A few minutes later we went out for the seventh set and I realised how hot it was in there. It was the middle of November and people were going outside to cool down. I could see people in the audience with shirts soaking wet with sweat.

We started the seventh set and something didn't feel right.

I suddenly felt like I was going to collapse. Phil went two-nil up in legs and asked me, 'Are you alright?'

'No,' I said. 'I'm fucked.'

Phil then threw his darts and went over to Russ Bray, who was doing the calling, and told him I wasn't well. As I threw my darts Russ asked how I was.

'There's something wrong. I think I'm going to collapse.'

Russ said we could have a break after that set, so I knew I was going to get off the stage for some air. I was two legs down at the time and you'd think I'd try to lose the next leg as quickly as possible to try to get to the break. But my fighting instinct kicked in and I ended up winning the next two legs to make it two-all. Unfortunately, Phil won the next one and so he was five-two up in sets.

I went off and John McDonald, the master of ceremonies, was there with a few other people. His wife is a nurse so he looked after me. I must have looked terrible. I heard later that Sid Waddell said on TV that I was sweating so much I looked like a 'hippo in a power shower', which isn't very nice but it's funny and probably quite accurate.

When I came off, John said they had to cool me down; they got my top open and lifted my t-shirt up. He took my pulse and apparently it was so quick that I must have had a really strong heart, because a lot of people would have had a heart attack at that stage. I told them to give me a few minutes and I'd go back out and play again. They took one look at me and said, 'No way, you're not going out there again.' So the game was called off and I sat down to cool off for a while.

I should have gone to the hospital after that but I didn't, because when I got into the car and sat down I ripped my trousers right round the arse, so I told the driver to take me home. I slept okay that night and when I woke up the next day I didn't feel too bad. So, me being me, I told myself it was just the heat and there was nothing bad going on inside me. I waited until I felt better later in the day and started drinking as usual.

I wonder now if I might have stopped myself getting into such a state a couple of years later if I'd gone to hospital that day. You never know – the doctors might have been able to get a grip on it. I was obviously already in a bad way but I didn't do anything about it. I didn't get any help and that was stupid, because it could have cost me my life.

Jenny

Andy was playing okay at the start of the game against Phil, but, as the camera went close-up on his face, you could see he was sweating heavily and his eyes were red and bloodshot. He looked terrible. After a while they went off for a break and it was announced that Andy would not be coming out again, as he was ill. Naturally I went to see what was wrong, and I found him sitting out at the back of the venue. People were putting ice on his head and back to try to cool him down. He was grey and we tried to get him to go to hospital, but he wouldn't. All he was worried about was letting people down – those involved in organising the game, the people who'd come to watch and me, because of the money. (Which he ended up getting anyway, so he didn't need to worry about it.) The next day Andy stayed in bed, still feeling rough. It was then that he had to make a big decision – what was more important, his health or his drinking? Unfortunately, he made the wrong choice.

TEN

FIT CLUB

In the middle of 2004, my manager called and asked if I'd be interested in going on a programme called *Celebrity Fit Club*. It sounded like my worst nightmare. After all, I was a shy, overweight darts player, not a celebrity. I knew I was unfit and I didn't want to humiliate myself in public. But my manager wouldn't give up.

'Are you sure you don't want to do it? It'll be a great programme.'

'No, I'm not doing it.'

'There's good money involved'

'No again.'

'It'll do you good.'

'It's still no.'

I was dead against it. But then Jenny got involved and between them they managed to talk me into it. I was still in denial about my health, so I didn't really see it as urgent. I know I was unfit but I didn't realise just how bad it had got.

Jenny knew though, and she hoped going on the programme would make me change my ways.

The first thing that happened was that one of the producers of the show came to see me for a chat. He was a nice bloke and he made the whole idea a bit less daunting. If I hadn't liked him I don't think I'd have got involved. I asked him a few questions, like why they wanted someone like me, because I didn't think anyone would be interested in watching me on telly if I wasn't playing darts.

'You'd be good on it, Andy,' he said. 'People will like you and it'll be good for your health.'

He seemed really keen to have me on the programme, so I thought, *Why not?* It wasn't going to do me any harm. The next thing I knew I was signed up.

A few weeks later I went along to where we were filming for the first time. I met the TV presenter Paul Ross, who's Jonathan's brother, and a few others, who all seemed really nice. Then I met Harvey Walden, the American fitness instructor I would end up spending a lot of time with.

Now, away from the cameras, Harvey was a very, very nice bloke. He'd also been a US Marine for 20 years and so was basically as hard as anything. He could be very scary when he wanted to, which was mostly when the cameras were on. What he does for TV, he does very well: he shouts and screams at people, but no matter how angry he seems to get he always says exactly the right things. He never fumbles or hesitates over his words, which is very impressive. Harvey is a very clever bloke. He reminds me of the guy in *Full Metal Jacket* who walks up and down yelling at the new recruits. If you've seen that film, you'll have an idea of what it's like being shouted at by Harvey – really rather frightening.

When I met Paul Ross I was also introduced to the show's host, Dale Winton, who I liked straight away. I'd met Julie Goodyear – who for years was *Corrie*'s Bet Lynch – the night before, when I arrived at the hotel where we were staying. Before I arrived, I'd been really worried about swearing in front of the other people, in case I offended them. Everyone who knows me knows I swear a lot. (There might not be much in this book, but that's because most of it has been taken out. Trust me – I swear in pretty well every sentence!) I didn't know how the others would react to this, so I thought I'd try to be on my best behaviour.

'Andy, how are you?' said Julie.

'Very good, thanks. How are you?'

'Oh I'm fine. But those papers, those fucking newspapers, they're such bastards to you, aren't they? And what about those fucking wankers who work for them?'

She gave them a right mouthful. I wasn't so worried about my swearing after that. But I was a bit confused – I mean, this was Bet Lynch and she was swearing even more than I did! We had a couple of drinks in the bar and a good laugh together straight away.

The next day filming started. At the beginning of the show they filmed everyone as we walked into a room and met the others. It was Paul Ross and Tina Baker that I got on best with; Tina, who's the soaps commentator for GMTV, was brilliant, scatty but very, very funny. When we went into the room they told us they were going to pick two captains and then the captains would pick their teams, so the whole programme would be based on two teams competing against each other to see who could lose the most weight. At first Julie was one of the captains, but they changed it and made famous Italian chef Aldo Zilli captain instead.

Aldo and Paul went and stood in front of everyone else. We were waiting to be picked, feeling like we were back at school again because no one wanted to be left until last – especially me, as I wasn't particularly happy or comfortable being filmed.

Paul picked first. 'I've never had a World Champion in my team,' he said, picking me before anyone else, which was great. It was only a small thing, but that really helped calm my nerves. Thanks, Paul.

After that we had to start the actual Fit Club, which meant a fitness test. We went over to a football pitch and then Harvey appeared. First of all we started doing some stretches and loosening-up exercises. I could barely reach the things he wanted us to stretch, let alone stretch them. I was not enjoying myself one bit.

Next Harvey told us we had to run round the football pitch under a set time limit. I looked at Julie and Julie looked at me. We were both very nervous. Then we both looked at Harvey, who could easily read our expressions.

'Okay,' he said, 'those of you who want to walk can walk. Remember we're doing this now to set a time so we can monitor how much you improve as the show goes on. Whatever you do now is fine.'

That made me feel better, so off we went. I was fine at the start . . . but not for long. By the time I'd got halfway round the pitch I couldn't breathe. I had completely stopped and was really struggling for air when suddenly I heard a voice booming out, 'You have got to be kidding me!'

I looked up and Harvey was bounding across the pitch towards me. I got my breath back eventually and carried on, but it was really, really hard. I think it took me about four and a half minutes to get around it in the end. It was

178

horrible. I couldn't even manage just one lap of a football pitch. I was gutted.

At that moment a little reality kicked in. I weighed 31 stone and was in serious trouble. I already I knew I was unfit, but until I went on *Fit Club* I didn't realise how bad I really was.

After that we went into the gym to do press-ups and a few other things. This time I had a genuine excuse. I'd broken my wrist not long before and was due to play Phil Taylor in our head-to-head match a few weeks later, so I couldn't do them. Christ only knows what would have happened to my wrist if I'd tried to put all that weight through it, so I put my hand up. The game against Phil was worth a lot of money to me and I said I wasn't prepared to put it at risk. I showed them the scars and they were happy with that, so I didn't have to do the press-ups. Then we came to the next round of exercises and I couldn't do that either. I was beginning to feel like a right idiot.

Harvey looked at me and said, 'Any more surprises for me?'

'Well, as it happens, yes. I've got a bad back.'

I've had a bad back for years. There wasn't a particular incident which set it off but over the years it's got gradually worse. Getting heavier and doing no exercise won't have helped much either. It meant that when we started at the gym I had to sit it out. I was relieved, to be honest, because I'd had enough of humiliating myself. *Fit Club* was tough in lots of ways apart from the physical stuff. Knowing people were filming and watching you at these difficult moments was very hard. I tried not to think about it too much, but it was embarrassing knowing I was going to be seen like this by all the viewers.

It was the first time I really began to understand what a state I'd got myself into with my drinking, and it upset me. So what did I do to cope with it? Did I clean up my act and work harder on my fitness, while listening carefully to every bit of nutritional advice I possibly could?

Did I bollocks!

No, my way of getting through the tougher days was to drink more. I also drank more when I had a good day, because I thought it should be celebrated. Looking back now, I can see how messed up I was. But then I just took it one day at a time. I didn't think any further into the future than getting through the day in front of me, and to do that I thought I needed to drink. I was a mess, although at that time I didn't realise just how much of a mess.

I enjoyed *Fit Club* overall. When we started doing the show we'd go there every week and you'd slowly get to know people. I enjoyed that. I liked some of the people a lot and it was good to build up friendships with them. But I didn't get on brilliantly with all of them.

One week, Lizzie Bardsley – who was on the first ever edition of *Wife Swap* – started to dig me out to the cameras, saying I wasn't trying hard enough and all that. Lizzie said I wasn't taking a full part in the show and was cruising along, doing what I wanted to do and taking it easy rather than sticking to what Harvey and the others wanted me to. But I wasn't. I'm no prima donna. I was trying my hardest all the way through. It's just that, for me, exercising like that was really, really painful. I just couldn't do it. Having a go at me wasn't fair.

If Lizzie had been sensible enough to realise what my size was doing to me, and to give me some support instead of knocking me, I think people would have taken to her a lot more than they did. I don't think people liked me for any other reason than they felt sorry for me, but that was enough to make me popular. I was the biggest and found it the hardest, so I was the underdog, the one suffering the most and the one people pitied the most. People always support the underdog, and Lizzie didn't realise that. She couldn't get past wanting to be centre of attention all the time.

She even said Harvey was in love with her. He got to hear about this and, when we were being weighed one day, he brought it up, asking her why she'd been saying it. Lizzie started defending herself, saying it wasn't true, but Harvey wasn't having any of it and said something which completely shut her up:

'Listen, if you were the last whale in the sea I wouldn't ride you to the shore.'

Me and Paul Ross absolutely pissed ourselves laughing. What a brilliant line!

I don't know exactly why she behaved like that, but I have an idea. A few of the people on the show were actors, or known for their personalities, and seemed to try to take that with them onto the programme so that they'd make more of an impact than if they were just being themselves. In Lizzie's case she was known for being blunt and outspoken from *Wife Swap*, so I suppose she thought she'd better do that to stand out. I just happened to be the person she picked to slag off.

I would never do that. I've always tried to be totally genuine and I can't be any different – not because I'm particularly nice but because I'm no good at pretending, I'm a bad liar. Some people might not like me – and there have been plenty of those over the years – but I've never tried to be anything other than what I am. At that time, I was a very fat bloke who drank too much. I might not have been brilliant at the exercises but I wasn't rude to her or anyone else.

Still, it made for good telly.

Aldo Zilli was a really nice bloke. Jenny and I went to his restaurant not long after the programme finished; we saw the Frank Sinatra show after having dinner at his place. The food was lovely and healthy, too!

On my team, Paul Ross was right behind me all the way through the programme and gave me lots of support, as did Tina Barker and Kym Mazelle, the soul singer.

After a month I started to enjoy doing the show. I'd got to know a few of the people, become friends with them and looked forward to seeing them. We went every week for the first month, then every two weeks after that so they could check our weights and keep track of how we were doing.

On the day of our first weigh-in, I was down at the gym at the Lakeside where I was playing in the World Championships. I was doing some exercise before heading over to where the programme was filmed. There weren't many people around but there was an old girl on the walking machine next to mine. The trainer said she was going to cover up the clock on the machine so I couldn't see how long I'd been going for, as watching your time apparently really puts you off. So I started and after a while I was really struggling, so I asked how long I'd been going.

The answer? About two minutes.

The trainer told me I had to do a bit more so I carried on. I got to four and a half minutes and I was in real trouble and had to stop. I looked over at the old woman next to me and she was giving it loads, going seriously fast. I saw her timer and she'd been going for about 45 minutes. I'd fallen to pieces after less than five minutes and this old girl had been hammering it for three quarters of an hour. Then, on the telly in the corner of the gym, an advert for the show came on and they used a clip of me sitting on a chair with my head bowed down, gasping for air. The old girl looked at the telly, looked at me, looked at the telly, looked at me again and then got on with her exercise, all without changing the expression on her face. It's very embarrassing to be shown up by a super-fit old lady.

After about three weeks, we went to get weighed for the first time since the show started. At the time I thought I was doing well. I'd stopped drinking beer and was on the white wine, like they'd told me to, and while there'd been a few moments like that with the old lady, I'd tried to use them to motivate myself rather than letting it get me down. I knew I had a long way to go but I'd done everything they asked me to for three weeks.

Then, when I went got weighed, I found out I'd lost half a pound.

I was devastated. I'd been trying really hard and that was the result. Half a bloody pound! I think they could see how disappointed I was. I'd done all that work for nothing. I started wondering what the point of carrying on with it was. After all that effort I'd lost half a pound out of 30 and a half stone, not even equal to a can of beans.

Jenny was with me, so they took her aside and told her to have a word. They said she should try to make sure I didn't feel too disappointed because they knew how important it was that I carried on and that, if I did, I would get results. The doctor said I might have been turning fat into muscle, because I'd done so little exercise over the past few years and as a result my muscles had got smaller. Now they were working again they had to grow to cope with it. When he told me this for the first time, I thought he was taking the piss and treating me like an idiot. I found out later it was probably exactly what was going on.

He and Harvey were on my case, so I decided to carry on. I liked them both, and Harvey wasn't always the scary guy you saw on the telly. He was a good man. The following week I went back and I'd lost nine pounds, which gave me a real boost. I told myself I'd just needed a while to get into the swing of all the lifestyle changes and the exercise routine.

That first bit of success helped me enjoy the show more. It was good fun and I had so much support that it felt unreal. People were getting behind me in ways I never expected. Before the show started, I'd be walking round town and a few people would say, 'Oh, there's that darts player.' Mostly older or middle-aged people, though they didn't really do it that much. But suddenly there were loads of people – mostly old women, actually – who'd come up to me and say, 'Aren't you doing well on that show?' and, 'Good luck, Andy!' So many people watched *Fit Club* it was amazing. Until you're actually involved in something like that it's hard to understand how big these things get. It was incredible, really amazing; even Dale Winton said that, everywhere he went, the first thing people asked him about was how I was getting on with the weight loss. It was nice that people cared so much.

Telling me something like that was typical of Dale, because he is one of the nicest blokes I've ever met and very funny too. He's also very impressive when you watch him work.

Every other presenter I've seen doing their stuff has had an earpiece which lets other people prompt them as they go along, but Dale doesn't. He does everything from memory and if he feels it's not absolutely perfect he'll stop and do it again. He's a real pro. He also loved Aldo and wouldn't stop cuddling him, which made me laugh.

While *Fit Club* was on telly it got a lot of publicity, which meant I was invited to all kinds of events. One time I was asked to give out a radio presenter's award at the Dorchester Hotel. On the night a car came to pick us up and, as we were driving along to the venue, there was a little brochure about the night from the year before on the back seat. Jenny was having a look through and it turned out to be one of those proper big awards evenings, with a huge stage, hundreds of people and tables, lights and so on.

I said to the driver, 'Do us a favour, mate, turn round.'

'What?'

'Turn round, we're going home.' I said to Jenny, 'You get on the phone to that woman who invited us and tell her we are not coming.'

'What's the matter with you?' she said.

'I am not getting up there in front of all those people.'

That kind of thing was my worst nightmare. I hate being in front of huge crowds of people when I have to talk. Even when I was drinking I hated those situations. Darts matches were just about okay, but this was about as far from my idea of fun as it is possible to get.

But eventually Jenny talked me into it, as she always does. We got there and someone thanked me for agreeing to present the award, and told us they'd come and get me 10 minutes before I was meant to be on stage. I was giving out the Sports Presenter of the Year award. All I had to say was,

'The nominees are,' but every time I tried to practice the words came out as, 'The knobbly knees are . . .' You know when you get a stupid idea in your head and can't get it out? That was me on that night. Now I was even more nervous.

We were sitting down at the table and suddenly this gorgeous woman appeared. She knelt down right in front of me. I thought I was dreaming. 'You probably don't know me,' she said, 'but I'm Nell.'

It was the model Nell McAndrew, so I said, 'Oh, I know who you are, don't worry!'

She said how well I was doing at losing the weight and how she knew someone in a similar situation. She was being really nice.

Out of the corner of my eye I could see Jenny looking at me. She was laughing at me, and said to everyone later, 'Poor Andy, you could see on his face how much he was cursing his luck, because the one time in his life he was ever going to get Nell McAndrew on her knees between his, he had his wife sitting right next him!'

A bit later Tom O'Connor came up to me.

'Hello big boy,' he said.

'Hello Tom.'

'I've got one thing to say to you.'

'Oh yeah, what's that?'

'You haven't won anything tonight!'

'Cheers Tom!'

He was really nice, very funny too. But then I had to go up and present the award. Tom was onstage with June Whitfield, and when they announced my name there was a lovely big cheer, with loads of clapping. It was a great moment, it made me feel really good.

As I went up the stairs there were three girls waiting for

me. I walked past them, took the envelope and then walked out onto the stage. By this time I was shitting myself about 'knobbly knees'. I got up onto the stage and just looked at my card. I knew that if I lifted my head up I'd go to pieces, so I kept my head down.

'The nominees [yes! Got it right!] are Jim Rosenthal, John Inverdale and [another one who I can't remember], and the winner is . . . John Inverdale.'

John came up, got his award and we had some pictures done. After that I went back to my table and, a bit later, Barry Cryer presented a special award for Ronnie Corbett.

Ronnie was right by me, only a few feet away. Everyone knows he's a very small man but I didn't realise just how tiny he was. He's a legend and I've loved his programmes for years, so I decided to say hello. I turned around and said, 'You don't know me, Ronnie, but I just wanted to say congratulations. I'm a big fan of yours.'

'Hello Andy,' he replied, 'thank you very much. Aren't you doing well at that *Fit Club*!'

I couldn't believe it, I was speechless. Ronnie Corbett watched *Fit Club* and knew who I was! I looked at Jenny and she was laughing. In the end I was glad I went along that night, but fuck me, was I nervous!

One of the weirdest things that happened around that time was meeting Robbie Williams, when I was working on a TV programme with Ant and Dec. He'd come on stage when everyone had to guess the price of a chocolate machine as part of the show. As you'd expect, all the girls were screaming and cheering at him.

In the VIP section afterwards he was supposed to be meeting MTV to talk about big business things, but apparently he said, 'I'm not having any meetings at all until I've had one with that bloke over there,' and pointed at me. He came over for a chat and gave me a cuddle. We talked about darts, *Fit Club*, his music, he was very nice and genuine, there was no flashness or anything like that. And he was surprisingly tall, too. It was a very weird experience.

I was supposed to go to the *Hell's Kitchen* studio once, not long after the programme finished, but I couldn't because I didn't feel well. I told the girl who booked celebrities for the programme I was too ill to come, but she wasn't having any of it. She said I had to because Liam Gallagher from Oasis was going to be there and wanted to meet me. Liam Gallagher wanted to meet *me*? It was amazing. She even said he'd rearranged his diary to be able to get along. But I couldn't go because I really wasn't well. That was a shame, because I'd love to have met him.

There were a lot of good things about being on *Fit Club* but it wasn't always fun. There was a big problem one evening at the hotel near the end of the show. Paul Ross was there with his wife and a couple of friends and they all went out for a meal. I was there with my mate Stevo and Ken Morley was around too, the comedy actor who used to play Reg Holdsworth in *Corrie*. Ken was on his own so I asked him what he was doing for something to eat. At the time we were friends and it's never good to leave someone on their own, so we were just trying to look out for him. Ken said he was going to the hotel restaurant, me and Stevo were doing the same, so I said he should come and eat with us.

We met at the bar where the maitre d' came in to give us our menus. We had a couple of glasses of wine each and then we were told our food was ready, so we went through. Ken had about three more glasses of wine while we were eating, which made about five so far. I was on the white wine spritzers like a good boy.

Just after nine we came out of the restaurant and went to the bar. Paul and the rest of them came back and we were all having a laugh. Ken had slowed down on the drinking and was slipping behind the rest of us a bit, so I got him a bigger glass. But that's all I did.

By now he was getting quite pissed. I know now how wrong it is, but at the time I wanted to see how pissed he could get. Well, he went to bed at about a quarter past 12 and he was hammered. He'd been leaning on the wall in the toilets to prop himself up, a real mess.

The next day he didn't turn up for *Fit Club*. By all accounts, he wouldn't come out of his room. What they did next was, I thought, bang out of order. They went into his room with a camera while he was lying in bed, apparently he was stark naked. They shouldn't have done that to him. Harvey, who'd gone up to try to get him to come out, quickly realised that and sent the cameras away. Then he got Ken out of bed and into the shower. It was the second to last day and we were going to an army base to do some kind of assault course, so it was important for Ken to be there.

We went to a pub for lunch first and I did a stupid thing. Ken hadn't turned up because he was so ill, so I put a glass of red wine in the middle of his place setting. Then I said to Stevo, 'I shouldn't have done that last night.'

Well, people picked up on that, and I think they thought I'd done something to Ken's drink. But I would never, ever do that to anyone. *Ever*. Whenever my kids go out I always make sure they have enough money to buy another drink if they think something has happened to theirs. I know from all our years running pubs how careful you have to be with things like that, and I'd never do it in a million years. But that didn't stop people from thinking I had, all because I said that stupid thing to Stevo.

Ken still hadn't turned up. Someone said he'd asked for some time to sort himself out and had gone up to his room before he was due to meet us downstairs. About a quarter of an hour later we heard this scream coming from upstairs. It was only a small hotel, so there wasn't far for the noise to travel; Harvey ran up to see what had happened and the girl who was waiting outside Ken's room was in a right state. She said his door had opened a little bit and she'd pushed it a bit further to see what was going on. Suddenly this person appeared with a black bag over his head, holes cut out for his eyes, making ghostly noises and waving his arms above his head, then ran away. As you'd expect, it made her jump.

She searched and searched but couldn't find Ken. They even phoned all the local cab firms to see if one of them had taken him anywhere. But there was nothing. He'd vanished.

Later that week he was in the paper, saying someone had spiked his drink that night. He also said the only people he was drinking with were me and my 'minder', Stevo. So I phoned him up.

'Alright Ken, how are you doing?'

'Fine, yeah.'

'What was all that drink-spiking bollocks in the paper about?'

'Oh, that was nothing.'

'You're not blaming me, are you?'

'No, no, not at all.'

'Good. Because I wouldn't do something like that.'

'I know that, Andy. I wouldn't think that.'

But then I kept on thinking about it and something in my mind told me to be worried. There was only one episode left for us to do, but I phoned up *Fit Club* and said I wasn't doing it because Ken had been out of order on account of what he said in the papers. I've done a lot of stupid things in my life and I've got a lot of people drunk – like Ant and Dec, which was unfair and wrong of me. But I have never, ever made anyone drink something they didn't know about.

I told *Fit Club* I wasn't going anywhere near Ken because of what he'd said, and that if he said it again it could have caused Jenny and me problems with the pub. She's the licensee and I'm not sure what – if anything – the licensing people would have been able to do about it, but still, it wouldn't have looked good for us. So the producers said, 'Fine, come along for the last show and we'll make sure he's out of the way by the time we all have drinks afterwards.' I said I wouldn't go anywhere near him during the show, and it was accepted.

When I got there, Ken was having his makeup done and I was in another room watching football on the telly. Next we started going in to be weighed. Ken went first and Dale Winton said, 'Ken, you weren't there the other day. What happened?'

'I think I was tampered with,' he said, or something like that anyway.

'What makes you say that?'

'I've got my evidence.'

I was sitting there wondering what he was going on about.

'Can we see your evidence?' Dale asked.

'No, I'll show you when I go to get weighed.'

I suddenly realised all the cameras were on me. Tina knew

something was wrong and I was getting wound up. I told her I could see what was coming. The producers can obviously hear what's being said through your mic and, the next thing I knew, they were talking to Dale and Ken. They all went off somewhere, came back and started asking Ken about his 'evidence' right in front of me.

On camera, they said, 'We think you should show your evidence now so Andy can put his defence up.'

I thought, *What do you mean, put his defence up? Defence for what?* I was getting really angry now. The evidence Ken was talking about was his bill from that night. So what did his bill say?

'You can see there that I had five glasses of red wine,' he said.

'Okay,' I replied, trying to keep calm, 'but what about my bill?'

'Well, I don't know about that.'

'Well, you should have fucking asked, shouldn't you? Mine's got another five glasses of red wine on it which you drank and about 29 white wine spritzers which I had.'

I was furious by now, really wound up. It all got a bit stupid after that. Paul Ross steamed into Ken because he knew exactly what had happened – Ken had drunk too much and was now blaming me, no more, no less.

I stood up and said to the producers, 'You can shove this show right up your arse!'

They tried to calm me down but I wasn't having any of it. I told them it was their show, not Ken's, and he shouldn't have been able to do that to me. Trying to stitch me up like that wasn't right. They let him make his accusation publicly, in front of millions of people, without warning me what was going on. That is *not* right.

I said I was off and left the building. We all had our drivers and mine was a guy called Mel. 'Mel, get in the car,' I said, 'we're going.'

I was being chased by the producers shouting, 'Andy, come back, come back!' but I wasn't interested. I took my mic off and threw it away. I said I wasn't coming back because I'd end up hitting Ken and it would make everything even worse. He was an old man, after all.

I got into the car and, the next thing I knew, the doctor was sitting in there with me. He asked me what had happened and I started getting quite emotional about it all. I'd had a really good time on the show and had done nothing wrong, so it was all really unfair. It was all so public too, which was partly why I got upset. I had no idea what people watching the programme would see or think.

So the doctor said, 'Okay Andy, let's go for a drink and calm down.' What? A *drink*? I thought he was joking, but he wasn't.

In the meantime Paul stormed out too and asked if I was okay. I said, 'No, but we're going for a drink. Fancy coming?' Of course he did. So the three of us headed round to the hotel where it all started and had a few drinks in there, before heading back.

The only person from the other team who thanked me for coming back was Aldo. The rest kept quiet and Julie Goodyear stuck up for Ken. I suppose it's inevitable that she would, because they'd been friends for a long time, but it annoyed me.

It wrapped up pretty quickly after that. Everyone went their separate ways. I didn't think much of Ken. It was a shame, because he was a really nice, funny bloke, but he turned on me when all I did was have a few drinks with him.

He should be old enough to look after himself and mature enough not to blame other people.

I was the least famous celebrity they had on the show, so they probably thought they could get away with that kind of thing. I was only a darts player while all the others had showbiz agents, and I was quiet a lot of the time, too – not with the other people, but I got a bit shy when the cameras were on. They probably thought I'd just take it and not give them much of a reaction. They were wrong.

The way it ended spoiled the experience for me slightly, because those were my only bad memories – apart from all the painful exercising, that is. But it definitely worked because I lost three-and-a-half stone during *Fit Club*, which lasted about three months. If I'd done it really strictly I think I could have lost five or six.

Before the last show they gave me two weeks to lose 10 pounds. That was after my row with Ken, so I went home and went on the piss on Saturday, stayed on the piss all day Sunday, went to the gym on Tuesday, then flew to Tenerife on Wednesday for a stag weekend. That was not a quiet time, I can tell you.

One of the lads who went told his missus there was a darts competition out there, and he was coming out with me to give some support. He'd phone her and say, 'Yeah, Andy's doing really well, he's into the next round,' and so on. I got back from the stag weekend on Tuesday, went to the gym on Wednesday and then didn't do anything on Thursday or Friday.

At filming on Saturday, I went to be weighed. The announcer said, 'Andy, two weeks ago you weighed 27 stone. Today you weigh . . . 27 stone.'

He was so shocked he went silent.

'Andy, what happened?'

I couldn't lie to him. 'A five-day stag do in Tenerife didn't help!'

My mate, the one who told his missus there was a darts tournament out there, was watching the show at home with her. At first I don't think she picked up on what I'd said, so he subtly changed the channel. But she made him change it back and, by the time they were watching *Fit Club* again, I was being interviewed by Dale Winton. They switched over just in time to hear him say, 'A five-day stag do in Tenerife? Imagine if it had been two weeks!'

She just looked at him and went, 'Stag do?'

Poor bloke. We didn't see him for a while after that. And he blamed me too.

After it finished I swore I wouldn't go back on the beer and would keep going to the gym. But it didn't last long.

One of the worst things I did after *Fit Club* came after I promised Jenny I wouldn't drink spirits unless I was playing darts. I think she knew in her heart that my health wasn't going the right way, so she was trying to get me to do something about it, even if only by cutting down on the shorts. So I promised I'd avoid them.

But I let her down. By then my drinking was pretty bad. In the pub, at the times when Jenny was upstairs, I'd be in the bar with three bottles of Pils in front of me. Most people would just say no to anything stronger than that, but I couldn't. After I'd had the beers, I'd then ask for brandies and vodkas and by the time she came down I'd have three or four empty spirit glasses in front of me. It was a bad thing for me to break that promise. Jenny deserved better.

I got what I deserved when I came to defend my World Championship in January 2005. As the previous year's winner, a lot was expected of me and I got a lot of attention from the media and a lot of pressure. I lost in the first round. It was one of the worst feelings I ever had in my darts career, down there with the absolute low points.

At the time, everything was going wrong. I had a manager who was pushing me more towards the TV stuff and my darts went so far downhill it was unbelievable. In my first round match, I played really badly, losing three-two to Vincent van der Voort. I was in tears on the stage that night because I couldn't believe how much worse I'd become. Only a year earlier I'd been the best, I'd beaten one of the best players in the history of the game and become the World Champion. Now I couldn't even get past the first round. I was devastated. First thing the next morning I booked a flight to Tenerife for Jenny and me, because I needed to get away. The newspapers got wind of it and the headlines the next day were 'Viking Flies to TenerGRIEF'.

The way my darts deteriorated over that year was very hard to take. Looking back on that time now, I can see why it happened. I wasn't concentrating on my sport as much as I should have done. I was doing too much TV and lost sight of the fact that the only reason I'd got to the level of fame I had was the darts, so that should always have come first, with everything else following. I should never have made the TV stuff a priority.

I got very down around that time because I didn't know what was wrong. I thought I was doing the right thing, but I wasn't. I missed tournaments to go on TV shows which I should never have done. I would be told there was guaranteed money to go on TV whereas the darts money wasn't guaranteed, so I thought I'd be better off choosing the shows. I wasn't practising much or playing often and when

I did throw a few I was rubbish. I started drinking even more because I was so unhappy. I could feel my life sliding out of control. The only way I could cope was to keep drinking. But that just made everything worse.

It was a horrible time.

ELEVEN

BACK FROM THE BRINK

In the 2006 World Championships, at the beginning of that year, I lost in the first round again. My darts was going down the tubes and so was my health. As usual, I coped by drinking as much as I could, enough to enable me to bury my head in the sand. But I couldn't stay in denial forever because I was about to get an almighty reality check.

By the end of the year all the good effects of *Fit Club* had worn off. After the programme finished it took about three months for me to get back to how I was before. The weight I'd lost through exercising and eating well started coming back on, and I was soon drinking as much as I ever did, if not more. The state of my darts was really upsetting me, and so we went to Tenerife for Christmas 2006 to have a relaxing time, and for me to get my head together before the next tournament in January 2007. We weren't settled at home either, which was stressing us all out. We'd left The Rose earlier that month and were planning on buying a pub in West Sussex and moving down there, but nothing was decided. Money was tight and the pressure was on me to start playing well again.

By this time, I'd become one of those people who other people did things for. If I needed my suitcase carried, someone would do it for me; if I needed a drink, someone would get it for me. It didn't do me any favours because I got even lazier and didn't realise exactly how much of a mess I was in physically. People were always nice to me and I didn't stop them. At the time I didn't think anything bad about it, I just liked being looked after. But if I hadn't let them, maybe it would have been obvious to me earlier that I had to do something about my health.

In Tenerife, I found I was so out of breath I could barely walk 50 yards. If we went 200 yards I would have to stop three or four times. I remember saying to Jenny, 'Something's not right. I don't know what it is but there is definitely something wrong.' But it wasn't a huge problem out there because we were on holiday and were meant to be relaxing.

I can't believe I was so stupid. Of course something was wrong – I weighed 30 stone and had been drinking constantly for the past 20 years. But I couldn't see that. I was still in denial. I would be getting up to go to the toilet in the night, I'd go five paces to the bathroom and then five paces back and would be gasping for air. I knew something wasn't right but I didn't let myself think the worst. I just thought I needed more exercise and so I just carried on with things.

We went home for New Year and then it was on to the Lakeside for the World Championship. On the day I was going to play my first round game, I was up at about 10am and I was due to play at ten past six that night. Before I even left my hotel room I'd had a few vodkas and brandies. At about 11am I headed down to the bar and started drinking there. I met up with Andy Goram and a couple of other guys. Jenny drove me over from the hotel to the venue, but the security guard wouldn't let her go right up to the door, which left me a bit of a walk to get there – probably less than 100 metres. As I got through the people waiting to get inside, I realised I needed to stop so I sat down on the first chair I saw.

'What's the matter?' Andy asked.

'I don't know.'

'Do you want a drink?'

'Yes, brandy.'

So Andy went off to get me a brandy. He thought he was helping me because that was what I said I wanted. By the time he got back I was in tears, just sitting there crying my eyes out because I felt like I'd had it. I thought I was going to die. I hadn't felt like that before and it was a terrible shock. Physically I had nothing left, no energy, nothing, I couldn't stand up or walk, I couldn't do anything. My body was giving up on me and shutting down. I really thought it was the end.

But I still drank that brandy. And that drink, at 5:40pm on January 8 2007, was the last one I ever had. Sitting there on that wall at the Lakeside with Andy Goram was when my drinking stopped. I didn't know it at the time, but that moment saved my life.

Eventually I stood up and walked through towards the players' bar. I could hardly breathe and had to walk very slowly. When I opened the door into the bar I saw people looking at me.

I saw Sam Hawkins of the BDO and told him, 'I can't do this.'

'Why not? What's the matter?'

'I don't know. I just can't do this.'

So they took me into the press room to get away from everyone. It wasn't the best place to go as the press were all there, so they took me outside. I sat down on a wall and couldn't breathe. Jenny came to see me and she said I looked grey. Jenny's sister Mandy was there with her son, Basil, who is asthmatic, so they gave me his inhaler but it didn't help. Barbara Leach, who co-owns the Lakeside, thought I was having a heart attack so she called an ambulance. I found out later that they sent two ambulances because I was so big they thought it would take more than two paramedics to lift me up.

I know that when the press chase a story they are only doing their jobs and I don't hold that against them at all. I have lots of friends in the press who have always been good to me. But that night I was wearing an oxygen mask, being wheeled on a stretcher through the players' bar and the main part of the venue, and all the time the cameras were clicking away. When someone is in that state, they should be left alone. There were even people from newspapers phoning up the pub, saying they were my doctor and trying to find out what was going on.

When I was in the hospital they asked if I wanted security by my room because there were reporters trying to get in. I've never had any complaints about the media other than on that night. Raymond was with us at the darts but Emily was at home watching it all unfold on telly, and it must have been horrible for her.

By now I was in Frimley Green Hospital and they were doing all sorts of tests. After an x-ray they told me there was so much fluid inside me it was pushing right up against my lungs, which was why I couldn't breathe, so the doctor got out this long needle – the longest one they had – and pushed it right through my back to try to drain the fluid to take the pressure off my lungs. But it wouldn't reach.

Jenny

At that moment I knew how he felt when I had cancer. It is a horrible feeling watching the person you love in pain and not being able to help, not being able to take the pain away and make them feel better. That was a very long night. I sat beside his bed just watching him, praying I would not lose him and trying to be calm and positive when I spoke to the kids on the phone.

I had a terrible night's sleep. The next day they said they had to put a tube in my body to drain the fluid. They couldn't do it the normal way because I was so big and so it went in at the side of my back. I had to sign lots of forms before they could do it because the procedure was so dangerous. I didn't really pay that much attention to what they said might happen. I knew they had to do something to help me, so I just signed the forms and let them get on with it.

The doctor did it and then put a bag on the tube with a tap. He told the nurse to keep an eye on it and turn it off to empty the bag that night, before I went to sleep a few hours later. They put it all on and the next thing I knew, the nurse said, 'Doctor, I think you should have a look at this now.'

'Oh dear,' he said. The bag was full and it had only been 10 minutes since it was put on. He thought it would be hours later that it would have to be drained but I was in a far worse state than he realised. I think they filled four bags before I went to sleep.

Without some of that fluid, I had the first good night's sleep I'd had in ages, which meant that next morning I didn't like waking up. I hate being woken up at the best of times, but when I'm in a really deep sleep – and this was the first of those I'd had in a long time – it's even worse. But, being as it was a hospital, they woke me early.

I heard a voice.

'Andy, wake up.'

'Why?'

'You need to take these tablets.'

'Leave them there and I'll take them in a minute.'

'Okay but don't forget.

'I won't.'

I went back to sleep. A while later it happened again.

'Andy, wake up.'

'What now?'

'We need to weigh you.'

'Why?'

'Because we need to know how your weight has changed.'

So I got out of bed and sat in this weighing chair. Then I went back to sleep again. Not long after that, I was woken again. Now I was getting very grumpy.

'Andy, wake up.'

'What now?'

'We need some blood.'

I slung my arm out of the bed without even opening my eyes.

'No, we need the other one.'

'Why? What's wrong with that one?'

'We need the other one.'

So I stuck out the other arm instead. After that I went back to sleep.

But it happened again.

'Andy, wake up.'

'Not you again. Can't you leave me alone?'

'No, you haven't taken your tablets yet.'

On and on it went and it drove me up the wall. I know they meant well and I had to do what they said to help me get better, but I was more tired than I'd ever been before and wanted to be left alone. I don't mean to sound ungrateful because the staff were amazing. It was just how I felt at the time.

But I was beginning to feel better. Without all that fluid in my lungs I was breathing more easily for the first time in years. Jenny said my head started looking smaller after the second day and she thought she was imagining things. But they carried on weighing me every day and it turned out she wasn't going mad. I really was losing weight fast. I lost pound after pound and gradually started looking like the Andy she'd met all those years before. It was only then that she began to realise just how big I'd got.

The nurses quickly realised how grumpy I was every time they woke me up and so they tried to avoid doing it. One morning Jenny came in and I was still asleep, so they told her it might be a good idea to leave me alone. She didn't take that very well, but there was no way she was going to let it stop her from coming in and waking me up. She was used to me being grumpy! I stayed in Frimley Green Hospital for just over three weeks and, during that time, they took about 18 litres of fluid out of me.

While I was there Jenny was staying at the Lakeside Hotel, which was much closer to the hospital than our home. Bob and Barbara Leach, who own the Lakeside, let her stay there for nothing and it made everything so much easier for us. It was a really kind thing to do.

There was something else on my mind during that time which made everything much, much harder. A very good friend of mine, Peter Stanlick, had died just before Christmas. He'd had the pub in Thamesmead where we live now, The Cutty Sark. I found out he'd died on Christmas Day, when we were in Tenerife, and it knocked me sideways. He was one of my best mates, someone I'd known for years and years through darts.

I'll never forget the moment I heard the news. We were sitting in our room in Tenerife and the phone went. I was told he'd passed away and I couldn't believe it. He was one of the funniest characters I ever met, always really bubbly and full of life, always enjoying himself and surrounded by happy people. He'd always be at the darts whenever he could get there, although he didn't make the final in 2004. To this day, I still miss him.

Part of the reason why I was so miserable in hospital was that I couldn't go to his funeral. He was on my mind all the time. I must have been a horrible patient because all I could think of was Peter being buried and I was very, very low. We'd lost another close friend, Duncan Frame, a few months earlier and Peter had been very depressed about that too. Losing Peter as well as Duncan was a terrible blow. But I got through it, although I still think about Peter all the time. It's one of the cruellest sayings, but also one of the truest – life goes on. I'll always think of him but I can't change what happened. I can't bring him back, though I wish I could.

After Frimley Green, I was moved to the Royal Free Hospital in London. They did a few tests on me and the doctors told me my liver was ruined. They didn't try to cover anything up, they gave it to me straight: 'Carry on drinking and you'll die. Stop and you'll have a chance.'

I'd been told years before that my liver wasn't in the best state but I'd ignored the warnings. Doctors told me I was drinking too much and not eating properly, but I didn't listen. I thought they said that to everyone, no matter how you treated yourself, and that I was just like all the rest, with no more to worry about than the average man. Now I know they were telling me the truth.

I was discharged from hospital on January 31 2007 and we went home to Jenny's dad's house. With everything going on around us, we never got around to buying that pub in West Sussex.

That morning, I'd fallen over on the way to the toilet because my left side went numb. I was talking weirdly as well. Jenny was very confused because I was speaking much more slowly and quietly than usual. She couldn't understand how a dodgy liver could affect my face.

Later on, Jenny had to go and get my medication from the hospital and so she left me at her dad's place watching TV. While I was there I spoke to Wendy, Jenny's sister, on the phone and she immediately called Jenny to say I didn't sound right. Jenny phoned the hospital and asked for the doctor. She told them what was going on and they said it sounded like I was having a stroke and that I needed to be taken in as soon as possible.

There was no one around to take me to the hospital, so between them Jenny, her sister Wendy, Raymond and my mum organised everyone and called an ambulance. Jenny's dad is deaf and by now he'd come back in the room with me. He was sitting there watching telly, with his special headphones on, and all this was going on around him – phone calls, me getting stressed and upset, Raymond coming in to see me – and the first he knew about it was when the doorbell went and the ambulance arrived. Before I got in the ambulance – and Jenny still laughs at me for this – I got the hairspray out and made sure my hair looked okay. Well, you don't know who you're going to meet in a hospital waiting area, do you?

Raymond called my parents to let them know what was going on and I was taken to hospital in an ambulance. I spent six hours in the general waiting area before seeing a doctor. I felt okay actually, just a bit uncomfortable in the bed, but I didn't really know what was going on. I was out of it really, what with all the drugs I was already taking because of my liver.

Jenny

I met them at the hospital and when I saw Andy's face I was truly shocked. It was drooping to the left and he couldn't speak properly. I know the hospital was very busy that night but I felt so sorry for him, because they put him in the waiting room in a wheelchair with a blanket over him. I must admit I lost my temper a few times with people coming up wanting photos and autographs. He finally got to see a doctor six hours later, who said it was a stroke and that they would send him an outpatient's appointment for their stroke clinic. He also said, 'Happy birthday,' because by then it was February 2 and Andy was turning 45 that day.

Andy stayed in bed a lot after that. He needed help up and down the stairs to the toilet as his left leg was very weak, so we set up a bedroom in the dining room as it was easier for him. He had lots of friends visiting and trying to cheer him up, but he was very depressed.

I spent the next few months lying in bed all the time and being miserable. With all that time to think, I went over and over everything that had happened to me and what had brought me to that moment in my life. I realised that everything I did was an excuse to drink. All the time, everywhere I went, everyone I saw, no matter what I did, I'd use it as an excuse to have a few drinks before, during and after whatever it was. I realised that the way I'd been living my life was complete bollocks, and that it was my fault and my responsibility.

In early May, we went to a barbecue at Jenny's sister's house and we had a blazing row. It started on the way down there when I said I might just have half a shandy and Jenny said it wasn't a good idea. When we got there everyone was asked what they wanted to drink and, before I had the chance to say anything, I had a Coke put in front of me. I was angry with Jenny and she was furious with me. That was midday and the next time we spoke was about five hours later when I said, 'Do you want to go home?' and she said yes.

We drove home together and she was crying in the car. When we got home it got worse and we both got more upset. There were a lot of tears that night. It might have been a good thing for us to get all these things out, but it didn't feel good at the time. I was confused and scared and being sober made it even harder to cope with.

Jenny
I knew it was hard for him to adjust to life without drinking and he wouldn't go to any help groups, so in the end I said it was him who chose to drink and so it was up to him to decide firstly if he wanted to live and

secondly how he wanted to live. I told him I would be there every step of the way with him and I could take him whinging and moaning, but his illness was his own doing. If he did not want to help himself, no one else could. I told him how lucky he was to have the choice of whether to live or die because a lot of people do not have that luxury. When I had cancer I got up in the mornings, put on my makeup and made myself face the world because I did not want to die. I wanted to fight, but that could all have been in vain because I had no control over my illness. Andy had control over his and if he wanted to carry on as he was before, then I would not be able to watch him kill himself. He would be on his own.

The next morning things were different. I realised that, after all the shit I'd put Jenny through in the past, I'd gone and put her through even more at the barbecue. I was in a right mess then. I couldn't do anything for myself. I was weak and at times couldn't even make it to the toilet in time, even though there were only about six steps to go. Every time I moved I was in trouble. Jenny was the one who looked after me and cleared up the mess, and it was suddenly clear to me that I'd done the worst possible thing I could in return.

I decided I didn't want to give up on my life because I had too much to lose. I realised that the only person to blame for the state I was in was me, plain and simple. It was my fault and my fault alone, which meant it was up to me to do some-thing about it. I didn't go to Alcoholics Anonymous meetings because I really couldn't see how listening to other people's problems would help me.

Instead, I relied on my friends and family and, above all, Jenny. I was so lucky to have her there to support me. Without her, I think it's safe to say I wouldn't be here now. I don't take her for granted anymore.

Jenny

The morning after my sister's barbecue Andy woke up a different person. He said that he had realised it was his own doing and that he was ready to face the world sober. It may have been a long, hard road, but we were going to walk it together.

Giving up drinking isn't easy when you've relied on it for as long as I did. You get grumpy and start digging at the people who are closest to you and who are around you the most. It's lucky for me that Jenny was strong and could take it. After that night, I slowly started going out again and catching up with friends. Jenny was brilliant. It was great to be out seeing people again and it was a positive step, but each time I'd get to a stage where I didn't want to be there anymore. Somehow Jenny knew exactly when I got to that stage and she'd appear and we'd go home. I'd look at her in a certain way and she just knew. As time went on, it gradually got better and better and I started getting used to being around people I used to drink with, but without actually drinking myself.

We were in a bit of a shitty state when we moved into The Cutty Sark in July 2007. All the money I'd earned had gone and everything was going the wrong way. Taking over a pub gave us a bit of stability and we needed that. We were lucky to get it really, because the pub did both of us a lot of good.

It was hard for the kids, too. When I first started taking

the tablets after I stopped drinking, my moods were terrible. They made me into a right miserable fucker, not at all nice to be around. I knew when the bad moods were coming on and I'd try to go to bed, so that I was out of the way and didn't make everyone else miserable too. After a while, I got better at controlling it. There were things which would get me going at first but I started being able to recognise the signs. Then I started fighting it and trying to keep calm. As I got better at that, things got easier all round. Before that, it must have been horrible for Jenny, Raymond and Emily.

Moving into a pub might not look like the best idea in the world, but I think it did me a lot of good. I was around people who were drinking from the start and that probably did me some good without me even realising it. If I'd stayed away from pubs and drinking completely, then going back into that environment might have been really hard for me. And I like pubs because there are always people around; spending a lot of time on my own wouldn't have suited me, especially when I was struggling with my health.

After I had the stroke, I had to go back for countless check-ups, brain scans and all sorts because it was taking me a while to recover. In July, four months later, we were in America for a Rangers convention. We went to the Everglades and had a ride on one of those hoverboat things. It was brilliant fun, flying around all over the place, but as I went to get off I found I had strength in my right leg but none in my left. It completely gave way. I ended up on my knees in front of the guy who'd taken us out. He looked at me down on the floor in front of him and went, 'Are you alright?'

212

'Well, I'm not fucking proposing, am I?' I said. 'No, I'm not alright.'

He helped me up after that.

We went to see my manager when we came back to England. He lived in Somerset and we were supposed to stay for a couple of days. We were out one night and I went to get out of a taxi and just fell over. I sat there for about half an hour but my head was all over the place, so I decided we were going home. He tried to make us stay but I'd had enough, so Jenny and me got our stuff and went. We were supposed to be there for two more days, but that was it.

The effects of the stroke got to be really embarrassing. I have a quiet voice usually anyway, but after that it got even worse. People could hardly hear me. I started noticing that anyone I talked to would have to lean in closer and closer to be able to work out what I was going on about. Then they'd keep asking me to repeat myself and it would get worse.

It got better slowly and as I got more confident I started feeling happier. But there were a few times – quite a few, actually – when I didn't want to be anywhere except in bed. I was lucky really. If it had been a full stroke instead of a minor one, that would have been it. My face had gone down on one side but it wasn't that bad in the wider scheme of things – I was still alive.

I also started having fun again eventually. One night in the middle of 2007, only a few months after I stopped drinking, Raymond and I went to see *An Audience with Al Murray*. There were lots of celebrities there, with a red carpet and everything – even Eddie the Eagle turned up! (Jordan and Jodie Marsh were there, and Murray called them 'tangerines' because of their fake tans.) Everyone was wearing suits and looking really smart, but I didn't know the evening was meant to be like that so I was there in my tracksuit trousers, the kind of thing I wear every day. I phoned up the woman who'd arranged it and said there was no way I was going in with everyone else, because there was a TV crew there filming the arrivals. She took pity on me and let us in the back way.

At first I felt really uncomfortable with all those people around. But once the show started I settled down, because it was brilliantly funny. At the end, everyone got a goodie bag and in it was a signed copy of his book, where he calls me a 'pub legend', a packet of peanuts, a packet of pork scratchings, a pint glass and a wine glass. It was a great evening and I was really glad I went, especially as I had Raymond with me. Laughter is definitely good for you!

I kept my head down that year and just tried to look after myself. The weight started falling off me and, when I appeared onstage at the 2008 World Championships, I ended up all over the papers when they compared photos of me in 2004 to those three years later. The difference was unbelievable because I'd lost something like 12 or 13 stone.

As 2008 went on, I started getting out and about more. Before I lost the weight, people would recognise me and I'd feel uncomfortable. Once I'd lost about 11 stone, I could see people looking at me, then they'd look away and then look back again and think, *No, it can't be him.* I got a lot of people coming up to me and asking, 'Can you settle an argument for us?' I'd ask what it was and they'd say, 'Are you the Viking, Andy Fordham?' I'd ask why and they'd point to someone and say either, 'He says you're not and I say you are,' or it'd be the other way around. So I'd tell them and make at least one of them happy.

But people were always nice to me, even after all this time. The first time I was on the telly for the darts it was so strange. I had little kids in the streets coming up and asking if I enjoyed it, then middle-aged and older people would come up and say, 'You've done well,' and all that. The range of ages was great, especially after *Fit Club*, and everyone was so nice. People would even tell me I looked younger!

As I started to get used to life without drink, I started to laugh a lot more than I did before. In the back of my mind I was obviously worried about the state of my liver, which was still in a terrible state, but I was happy with the way things were going and tried my best to enjoy myself.

I don't have lots of happy memories from when I used to drink, but when I started doing things without alcohol I could enjoy them and remember them. We went to see the musical *The Rat Pack* in the summer of 2008 and I loved it. It was a great show but before, if I'd gone to see it, I probably wouldn't have remembered anything because the first thing I'd have done would be to get a drink. I'd have sat down and probably fallen asleep. Without drink, I could watch the whole show and have good memories of it. I realised I was a lot happier without alcohol. Jenny says that I laughed and smiled a lot more and, for the first time in ages, I started looking forward to the future.

I always said that, from the moment I stopped, it was simple: I just knew I couldn't drink again, ever, if I wanted to stay alive. People asked if I wanted to go to Alcoholics Anonymous or something like that, but I said no. I couldn't see how listening to someone else's problems would help me stop drinking. If anything, I'd get so depressed I'd want to take them out for a drink to cheer them up!

If I couldn't do it on my own then I couldn't do it. I've had loads of support from friends and family but no professional help, other than the doctor telling me that if I didn't stop I'd be dead in five years. That worked for me.

Now I was off the drink, I had two things to focus on – getting healthy and starting to play darts again.

TWELVE

EMERGENCY

In the summer of 2008, I heard the news I was dreading: my liver was so far gone I needed a new one urgently. If I didn't have a transplant, I would die because mine was so screwed up it was on the brink of failing. I was immediately put on the transplant waiting list, which meant I had to be ready to go as soon as a liver became available and had to be within two hours of home all the time. I was desperate to get a new liver but I tried not to think of where it was going to come from. Someone would have to die for me to live.

But I couldn't help dwelling on it, because after a while I felt like I was in prison and I hated it. Even though you can go a long way from home in two hours, it was still very hard to cope with being told I couldn't go far away – on top of the fact that I knew that, unless I got a new liver, I was going to die.

After two months of this I was at the end of my tether. Jenny and I went out to the pictures, but when we got there the film didn't start for three hours. So we went for a drive out into the countryside, just to get away for a while. We were driving along and I looked at my phone, just to check it. I didn't have any signal so I said to Jenny that we'd better get into town in case someone called.

By that time it was always on my mind. I could hardly think about anything else because I was so worried about it all. On the way back I decided I couldn't be bothered to go to the cinema. I wasn't in the mood anymore so we went back to the pub. We parked up round the corner because Jenny needed to go to Morrison's to get a few things. Off she went and I sat in the car waiting, too grumpy to get out and help.

Then the signal on my phone came back.

I had missed calls, text messages, messages from the pub, messages from other people saying that the pub was trying to get in touch with me, messages from the hospital, dozens of them.

I don't know how many messages I'd already listened to when I heard the words, 'The ambulance is coming. They think they've got a liver for you.' I immediately looked out of the window and saw Jenny sprinting across the car park towards me.

The funny thing was – and I didn't know this at the time – Jenny got the messages on her phone when she was right at the front of the queue in Morrison's, with her shopping unloaded and waiting to be put through the till. So when she heard there was a transplant for me and an ambulance on the way, she said, 'I'm so sorry, I've got to go,' spluttered something about 'liver' far too quickly for anyone to understand what she was going on about and just sprinted out, leaving her shopping there.

EMERGENCY

We were only two minutes away from the pub and, when we got in there, all the lads were being really weird and quiet. Normally there's a lot of noise in there but not today. They all looked terrified, I'd never seen them like that before. I didn't know what I'd be like when it happened, but I actually felt quite calm. I didn't think I could be like that but maybe their being so nervous made me calm.

I was standing there, my bag was ready and all the lads were asking, 'Are you alright?' I was fine, exactly the same as I'd been for the past few months when they treated me as one of them, the same as they always had. Now suddenly there was a liver transplant waiting for me and everything changed in their minds. I decided to do my best not to worry about it, getting stressed wouldn't make things any better. Having the lads do my worrying for me probably helped.

The other factor was that I'd been waiting for this moment for a long time. Over the past few months it had ruled my life, controlling where I went, what I did, causing me all kinds of stress and worry. Now the moment was finally here I was relieved that the waiting was all over.

The ambulance arrived with a bloke and a woman paramedic, and they were very calm. I asked them to park the ambulance around the back of the pub because it was a bit closer and Jenny had to carry my bag. I couldn't even do that for myself. They took my blood pressure and off we went. Normally it takes us an hour to get to the hospital from Thamesmead, but that day, with the sirens and lights on, it took less than 15 minutes. Those paramedics know how to drive.

We were coming from one direction and the liver was coming from somewhere else. The doctors want the two of you to arrive at exactly the same time, so as we got to the hospital I was taken up to the transplant ward. The doctor came in and started saying a few things about taking blood and so on. The nurse came in with all the kit, including the drip to put in my arm, and was just getting ready when her bleeper went. She told the doctor someone wanted to have a chat with her so the doctor left the room. Five minutes later the co-ordinator, Sarah, who I knew really well from previous visits, came in and I thought she was going to burst into tears.

'Andy, I'm really sorry but the liver isn't suitable after all.'

She thought I was going to be really upset but I just went, 'Oh well, fair enough, you told me it could happen. It's just one of those things.'

I didn't feel anything when she said that, not disappointed or relieved, nothing. The liver could have been too small or maybe not strong enough. There could have been all kinds of reasons, there was no point getting annoyed about it because it wasn't anyone's fault. I don't think it would have been the blood type because that's the first thing they look at, so it was probably the size. In the end the worst part was when she asked how Jenny and I were going to get home – we obviously hadn't brought our car, so we were stuck.

At the time we were filming for a BBC documentary about my liver transplant. They were based in Bristol, which meant when I got the call about a liver being available we'd have to move so quickly there was no way they'd be able to get there in time to film us on our way to the hospital, so they gave us a camera to use. Jenny was in charge of it so we called it the 'Jennycam'. All the way there the Jennycam was capturing it all, which made it all even more weird.

EMERGENCY

When we got into the room Jenny turned it off. We were talking to the doctor and asked if she minded us filming. We told her the BBC were going to film the operation and it had all been arranged. The doctor said it was fine as long as I didn't mind being asked personal questions on camera. That didn't bother me so away we went.

A couple of minutes later, while me and the doctor were having our serious chat, I heard, 'What's the matter with this bloody camera? How am I going to win an Oscar with this?' The doctor was trying to be really serious and Jenny was swearing about the camera. Just another strange moment on a very strange day.

Once we knew the liver wasn't right we just went home. My dad came to pick us up. I couldn't relax after we left the hospital. Before it I'd been quite calm, but when I had a bit of time to think about what had happened that day it shattered my composure completely. Just before we left the ward they told me I was now top of the list for a transplant. I was on code red. From then on, every time the phone rang –my phone, Jenny's phone or the pub phone – or someone said my name, I thought, *That's it, there's a liver for me.* I was on edge all the time. Being called in once on a false alarm made it real.

About a week later I went to see the doctor for another check-up and some more tests. I also spoke to her about how my blood was doing and she said it was improving. She also said that if I needed to change the dosages of the pills I was taking she'd phone me later that day to tell me. I didn't take much notice of this at the time. With everything else that had gone on it didn't seem all that important. But things appear a bit different when you look back on them further down the line.

Later that day Jenny and I were in Makro's and my phone rang. It was my doctor and I thought she was going to tell me something about the tablets. But she started talking about my blood and scans and other things, and as usual I didn't pay much attention. I never do – Jenny's the one who remembers the details. I wasn't really listening, then suddenly I heard her say, '. . . because you might not need the transplant yet.'

That got my attention. She was telling me other things but they weren't sinking in. Jenny was looking at me and I was trying to tell her what the doctor had said, but all I did was confuse her. As far as I'd been concerned I needed a new liver, full stop. I thought mine was so far gone there wasn't any hope of it getting even slightly better – that was what I'd been told all along. Now, suddenly, things had changed and I didn't know how or why.

The trouble was I wouldn't find out for certain what was going on for another week, when I'd go back to see the doctors again. To be honest, Jenny and I were both a bit annoyed about that because all we knew for that week was that there was nothing definite about a possible time scale. It didn't seem very fair to give us so little information at that stage, because it meant we spent the whole week even more stressed than usual. It was horrible not knowing. We'd get our hopes up and then start worrying again. It was a bad week, very tense.

Eventually the day came when we'd find out. We saw a different doctor this time, and he said my liver had improved so much I didn't need the transplant for another three to five years. I definitely still needed it, but it was no longer an emergency.

So, just a few weeks earlier I'd been in hospital about to

have the operation then suddenly, a matter of days later, I didn't need it anymore.

I was stunned. It was amazing news. It had been a confusing and difficult time, but I felt happy more than anything else. I felt like I'd really achieved something for me and for all the people who'd given me so much support, especially Jenny. I was proud too that I'd stayed off the drink for that long, stuck to my diet, taken my pills and done the right thing. I'd have been dead by now if I hadn't stopped, without question.

I looked at things completely differently after that news. I felt like I'd been set free in a way. Before that, if I'd started to feel a bit better I didn't think anything of it because I knew things were going to get a lot worse. A liver transplant is a huge operation and I had no idea what kind of effect it would have on me. All I knew was that recovering would be long and difficult, and there was no telling what kind of life I'd be able to have. All that changed when I was told I didn't need the transplant for three to five years.

Then, 10 months later, I was told I might never need to have it at all. Somehow my liver had made a more dramatic recovery from serious damage than anything the doctors had seen before. There may be a few different reasons for this. For one, when I stopped drinking in 2007 I really stopped. I never had any lapses so there was no more alcohol in my system. Another reason was that I didn't smoke and never had. If I'd got into the state I was in and had been a smoker, the damage to my heart and lungs would almost definitely have meant I wouldn't survive. But because I didn't smoke, my heart and lungs were relatively healthy so I had a slightly better chance of recovery. I'd also stuck religiously to my healthy diet and taken all my pills. For that, of course, I have to thank Jenny. She made sure it all happened.

* * *

At the end of 2008 I had a new lease of life. I was down to about 17 and a half stone and most of the fluids which had built up inside me had gone, so I could start doing a bit more exercise. I decided to get my back sorted and do my best to get back to playing darts. I felt great and couldn't wait to get started.

If I'd had the transplant with a suitable liver I might have been on the road to recovery by now; but then again, it's a major operation and could have killed me. My outlook now is that what happens in life happens. You just have to get on with it. There are things you should worry about and things which aren't worth the hassle. I became far more laidback than I used to be before all this started going on. My new view on life is that anything could be around the corner, so you just have to take each day as it comes and enjoy it as much as you can. That's how I try to live now.

There were so many things I could have done in the past but didn't, because I thought I wouldn't enjoy myself. Going to the theatre, football matches, I missed out on all kinds of things. You only know if you try and that's what I wouldn't do before. I was very stubborn, but I don't know why. I could have had so many great times with the people who matter most to me.

I like going to boxing nights now. A few years ago I wouldn't have gone because I'd have been nervous about meeting people. Now I go along, enjoy the evening and I'm happy to talk to people. I'm happy being me and if people like me, they like me. If they don't, they don't.

With my health improving I needed to earn a living, so I started trying to play darts again. The biggest problem straight away was confidence. I used to get nervous playing when I was drinking, but the alcohol calmed me down. Without it, I was terrified I'd be useless. So I needed to not worry about what other people thought and remember that I was doing it for myself and for Jenny. I had to convince myself I was still good enough to play properly, I just needed to rediscover the touch. The healthier I became and the better I felt, the more I practised. And the more I practised the better I got. The confidence to go up there and play without alcohol was still a long way off, but I was improving.

The only downside was that the BBC documentary about me was cancelled when they found out I no longer needed the transplant. I was annoyed about that, because I was earning much-needed money from it, and Jenny, my manager Steve and I had put a lot of time and effort into it. But then, as soon as there wasn't the drama of the operation to film, they weren't interested anymore.

As I got healthier, I started finding it easier to meet people and talk. My confidence started to get better. Before, I was embarrassed about my size and I'd want to walk in somewhere, sit in the corner and hide away. Drinking made it easier to do that. I knew that if I needed to go to the toilet I'd have to ask people to move out of my way, and that was embarrassing. I knew they'd start thinking, *Look at that fat bastard*, and I hated it. That would make me more anxious and so I'd drink more to get the nerves under control. Of course, the more I drank the bigger and unhealthier I became. It was a vicious circle.

I look back now and it's like looking into someone else's life. I can see a lot of places where I went wrong and things

I did wrong. It's a shame I couldn't have got out earlier and then gone back into darts, but at least I'm getting better now.

One of the best things about playing darts again is seeing my mates. When I started playing again I began seeing the same boys as before, like Monky (Colin Monk) and Jenks (Andy Jenkins). It was so good to be back with them again, I'd missed the banter and the fun so much. It's different to the old days because I'm not drinking, but that doesn't matter because I appreciate it so much more now. Jenny says she hasn't seen me smile so much in years.

Every time you talk to Jenks you end up in stitches because he's an absolute lunatic. He's been making me crack up for years. We went for a Chinese one Saturday night in early 2009 and then bowling afterwards. I couldn't bowl because of my back, so I had the pleasure of watching him get more and more wound up as Monky beat him at everything. Jenks has to have a bet on anything and all night, with everything he did, there was a fiver on it with Monky: pool, bowling, air hockey. Monky kept on beating him and Jenks was hating it. Every time they came back from playing some game Monky had his arms in the air and Jenks was raging about how close he'd come to winning. During the bowling Jenks even had a bet on his missus beating Monky's missus. The girls didn't have a clue what was going on until Jenks started having a go at his girlfriend and telling her how crap she was at bowling. Jenks was losing again, it just wasn't his night.

I know it doesn't sound like much, but I laughed so much that night. Simply being out with my mates again was something very special to me. There have been a few times like that recently, where I've seen some of my really good old mates and had a great crack. It's been so long since I've been able to do that, so it's great to be back. And I was actually enjoying myself without a drink in front of me. That made it even better.

Playing in the PDC, who I signed for at the start of 2009, is a different experience to the BDO. I went to see their tournament in Brentwood, Essex, to see how they did things, before I played one at Coventry the next week. I saw a few people and told them what I was planning; everyone was so positive and welcoming that, even though I was nervous, I didn't want to let them down. That support was great.

When I started playing in Coventry the next weekend, a few people came over to see what was going on, but it was nothing like being up onstage which was good for me. I wasn't ready to get back up there properly, so easing myself into it gently was ideal. I knew I wasn't going to be anywhere near as good as I used to be, and I was right. I was rubbish. But the important thing was to get back to playing again, to give myself a start and somewhere to build from, something to aim for.

After I got that first weekend out of the way and people realised I wasn't going to be right up there with the best players as I used to be from day one, it got easier for me. Getting over that hurdle helped me feel comfortable because the expectations were lower and more realistic. A couple of weeks later I played against Wayne Jones in Holland and he beat me six-nil, but it was the best I'd played so far. He turned round to me afterwards and said he took no pleasure at all from beating me and that he hoped I'd get back up to somewhere near the standard I achieved before, which was very nice of him.

Gradually, I could feel my head getting better. I started feeling more confident and comfortable with life. I even saw a hypnotist and she said everyone has a voice in their head that tells them things, and mine just seems to put me down. What she wants to do is turn that around so that my inner voice says positive things which make me feel more confident, rather than coming out with negative stuff all the time. If you can improve that and start thinking positively, then who knows what might happen?

When I started playing again, the support I got from my friends was incredible. Dave Ahmet, in particular, has been out of this world. He started helping me out recently, paying for me to enter tournaments not for any financial gain for himself, but because he wanted to see me back up there playing the big ones again. I am so touched by generosity like that. People have been so good to me since I started back that I've been amazed by it.

Apart from helping me sort my life out, the way people have treated me has made me want to do as much as I can to support a charity which has always been important to me, The Heart of Darts. It was set up by a great guy, Ian Waller, and his wife Joan, who do an amazing job. I'm an ambassador for it and Jenny co-ordinates their appeals. The Heart of Darts is a 'last resort' charity which supplies equipment people can't get through Social Services, the NHS or other charities, including things like wheelchairs, special beds and lifts for people who have trouble moving around. The majority of beneficiaries are children. After the health problems Jenny and I have had, and the incredible things that people did for us, I want to give something back now more than ever before.

At first, playing darts felt like starting from the very beginning again, and not just because I kept getting beaten all the time! 30 years ago, when I first played darts, I fell in love with it firstly because I liked hanging around with my mates, then I started enjoying the game more and more; then, when I realised I wasn't bad at it, I wanted to get as good as possible. At the start of 2009, I was beginning to feel that way again. I was enjoying practising because I could see little improvements every week. I started hitting more treble 20's, my doubles started coming more easily.

When the positive signs appeared, I started getting excited again. I was looking forward to going away and playing because I knew I'd have a laugh with my mates, but also because I was enjoying the challenge of getting my game back to a decent standard. I didn't know how far I'd get, but I knew I was improving and that was enough to get me in a positive frame of mind. After everything that had happened over the past couple of years, it was a great feeling.

It was extremely weird to be doing it without booze. At my first PDC tournament, in Coventry in February 2009, I was more tempted to have a drink than I'd ever been before. I went to the tournament early with George Noble, who was one of the referees and so had to be there before all the players. The place was empty and right in the middle of the room was the bar. I was a bit nervous about the day ahead and didn't have anything to do other than wait for everyone to get started, so I just sat down.

From where I was sitting I could see all the bottles there behind the bar. I saw the vodka and the brandy and I felt like they started waving to me, telling me to come over and say hello. For a moment I felt like the old Andy was back again, the one who'd go up there and drink everything he possibly could as quickly as he could. I started thinking that maybe, if I only had one, it might affect my head a bit more than one would have done in the past because I hadn't drunk for so long. Then I could have a glass of water to wash the alcohol through my system and still feel the effects in my head. That would help me get through the day.

I told all that to Martin, who owns the Cutty Sark pub, and he said it was insane thinking. But I then told him what I'd thought straight afterwards, that if I had one and it didn't work, I'd have to have another one and then another one after that, and I didn't want to start going down that road.

'You're lucky,' Martin said, 'because that second bit, the sane thinking, is the bit a lot of alcoholics don't have. They can't stop themselves from having another drink. They can't do it. You're lucky to have something which stops you from doing it.'

That moment showed me that, no matter how well you think you're doing, even if you think you've beaten it, the urge to drink is still there in you somewhere. Since the few weeks straight after I stopped drinking, when I really wanted one so much I didn't know what to do with myself, that moment was the hardest, the closest I came to throwing it all away. I hadn't drunk a drop for more than two years, I'd lost loads of weight, my liver was recovering, I was enjoying my family and my darts was improving, but the temptation was still there. It was the first time I'd been back in the place where I used to do most of my drinking – at darts tournaments – so it's no surprise I was tempted. But I got through it and I was proud of myself for that. I knew I had too much to lose.

I won my first match since 2007 in March 2009. I played in Coventry, Holland, Taunton and then Derby, where I beat a guy six-four. I played two in Coventry, two in Holland, two in Taunton, lost them all and then won my seventh game. I wasn't expecting to win, even though every week something had kicked in, something had improved. I felt like I was releasing the dart right or my throw was flowing and it was a matter of waiting for them to all happen together. Another time I realised I wasn't holding the dart in exactly the same way as I used to, and so I changed back to my old grip and that worked better. The improvements were all very small and gradual, but when they were added up it meant my game was heading in the right direction and, if I managed to get all those little improvements working at the same time, I'd be onto something.

I started relaxing a bit more. I could see myself getting better so I said to myself, *Try to win one*. That was what I really wanted. To beat someone again would give me that bit more confidence and the belief that I could actually be a proper player again and wouldn't be living off the things I'd done in the past. Don't get me wrong, I can handle that because I have to earn a living, but I'm a competitive person – that's what made me good at darts. As I started feeling better, healthier, that drive started coming back.

The best players are focused and driven and, while I could feel my enthusiasm building up again, it would have meant nothing if I was going to lose every match and never be anywhere near as good as I used to be. This game didn't make me think I was going to get back up to my old standard – that was still a long way off – but it was great to know I could win again. After eight legs we were even at four-four and then I won the next two legs. It was a great feeling because winning means a lot to me. It didn't matter that he wasn't one of the big names. He was a decent player and I never underestimate anyone. To me, darts is like that – anyone can beat anyone else on their day. That's how I've always prepared for matches, trying not to fear any player more than any other and to concentrate on my own game instead. So moments like this one are special.

Everyone was nice to me and would have been even if I'd been rubbish. No one gave me any shit and all I got was support. I was lucky really. They were telling me they were glad I was playing again and that they hoped I'd get back to some kind of standard. And then they left me to get on with it, which was exactly what I needed.

I didn't know what to do when I'd won that game. Back in the days when I was with the BDO, you would go back to the table where the officials were sitting and tell them the result so they could put the winner through and carry on organising the tournament. But this was my first win since I'd started with the PDC, and they do things differently.

They have four officials, each in charge of a group of players and keeping an eye on all their games. As I walked back after my game, the official in charge of us asked me if I'd won and what the score was. I told him, and he told me to sit down and wait for my next one, which I did. That was when it started getting strange. People were coming up to me, asking how I'd got on, and I was telling them I won, which seemed to shock everyone else almost as much as it shocked me. I hadn't said those words for so long that it felt really weird.

The official said he would come over and tell me when I was playing next and I sat there in a daze. The fact I'd won a game didn't really sink in. After all the troubles I'd had over the past couple of years, I'd beaten someone for the first time. I probably looked confused on the outside, but inside I was smiling.

My first win didn't make me think I was going to win the

World Championship again, but it gave me confidence and made me realise my darts was heading in the right direction. But that day, straight afterwards, I quickly found out I still had a long way to go.

There was a big challenge coming up immediately afterwards, because I was playing James Wade in my next match. I was really chuffed with that game too. Everyone knew I would need a miracle to win because James is a great player, one of the best two or three in the world, and was on great form at that moment. To be honest, I would have been happy to have won one leg and for it to have ended six-one. All I wanted was to not be humiliated, not to go down six-nil, because then my recovery would have meant nothing against the top players. I wanted to know I could mix it with the best again, and to take even one leg off a really top player like James, only a few games after winning my first match since my comeback, would have made me very happy. Luckily, I did even better than that.

First leg of the match and it was mission accomplished. I didn't do anything spectacular, just threw solidly with the darts and finished it off. Then my competitive streak came out and I thought to myself, *Wouldn't it be great to win another one?* James won the second with the darts and then I won the third. I'd taken two legs out of the first three, which felt brilliant. That was the moment I really started enjoying it. But he's a top player and can turn it on when he needs to, and so the next three went to James, leaving me four-two down.

At the end of the seventh leg I had a chance to do something special. James had left himself a double and I had 87 on the board, a finish I don't think anyone would have expected me to get. I went for treble 17, planning to leave myself a double 18 and the chance to win the leg in two darts. But I missed the treble and hit a single 17 instead, which left me 70 to get.

Even fewer people would have expected me to get the finish after that. Next was the single 20 – an easy shot, which I got. Then I had the bull for the final 50 points and the chance to take the leg in a way no one would have expected me to.

I didn't panic and I didn't think about that dart being important for any reason other than getting me back into the match. None of what happened in the past two years went through my mind. I didn't think about the significance of proving myself against one of the best in the world again, I didn't think about what this performance might mean for my future matches. I was just there, in the moment, playing the match. I felt like a player again.

And yes, I got that bullseye to make it four-three. I turned round and, as I walked back, I winked at James. He smiled and said, 'This is not in my game plan, you know.'

I had him rattled. One of the best players in the world had been knocked off his stride by me. I really was getting somewhere.

But that didn't stop him beating me. He was too good and I ended up going down six-three. I didn't like losing and I knew there was still a big gap between me and the very best players, but I was happy. It wasn't a huge moment for anyone else – it wasn't a major tournament and there weren't many people watching – but it meant a lot to me. After all the low moments I'd had over the past two years, having a high point like that made a very welcome change.

He's a good lad, James, and a really top player. I like him

a lot, even when he beats me. He told me afterwards that I frightened the life out of him at that moment, because he didn't expect it from me. To tell you the truth, neither did I. I'd made some plans in my head about when I thought I might start winning a few games again, but it wasn't that early. Even when I was being optimistic I was only really hoping for late 2009, because I didn't know how much I'd be able to improve or how quickly I'd be able to make it happen, if at all. I don't know what the future will bring for my darts. Maybe I'll get back up there, maybe I won't. My worry is that without the drink I won't be able to take the pressure, because in the past that's the thing which helped me cope. Time will tell. But at least I'm happy. I've got a new manager, Steve Mottershead, who is looking after me brilliantly and there is a new world of opportunities out there for me.

I've thought about what it would feel like to be up on the stage playing the big boys again. I've had a few nice little daydreams about what it would be like to walk into that atmosphere and hear everyone cheering for you, how it would feel to have that again. I've already worked out the music I'm going to walk into – 'Rock and Roll' by Led Zeppelin. That would be great, but there's a lot of work left to do. I just need to get some consistency. I'm trying to throw every day, an hour's practice when I can, or when the lads are around I'll play until whenever.

If I'm on my own and I'm not throwing well, I start thinking about all kinds of things – like how my arm is moving, my wrist, how I'm holding the dart, if my head's in the right place, all sorts, and I end up in a right state. But if I just relax and get on with it, I'm much better. It should be a natural thing, your darts throw, and when I start analysing it

235

too much I struggle. Drinking used to help me stop thinking too much. Without it, everything is brand new and far more complicated, so I'm coming back a totally different person to the one I was before.

I'm not the same darts player either. My hands are smaller now I've lost all the weight, and that means I hold the dart and throw it differently to how I used to. I even play in a jumper now because I get cold in the big halls where the games are. That didn't happen when I was drinking.

Looking at my future in darts, my ambitions are simple. I want to be playing against Taylor, Barneveld, Wade and the others – not necessarily becoming World Champion, I'd just love to be in there. But, with a bit of luck, you never know what might happen.

Over the years I've become a big fan of boxing. I love it because it's about two men up against each other and nothing else. Once they're in the ring, no one can help them, they're on their own. There are two basic different kinds of boxers: the ones who have the skills to get out of the way of the other guy's punches and still get their own in, and then the fighters, the guys who steam in and throw their punches while getting hit at the same time. I tend to like the tryers more than the really skilful ones, someone who's got the guts to hang on in there rather than beating someone else easily. I like to think of myself as one of those types – someone who's taken a lot of punishment but has fought back.

I'm proud of where I am today and how I got myself here, but I know how lucky I've been. I played a silly game with my life and was very fortunate to get away with it. My illness was entirely my fault and it nearly killed me. Only *nearly*, though. I'm still here, and from now on I'm going to make the most of everything in my life.

EMERGENCY

On July 20 2009 I was told that, if I carry on looking after myself and doing what the doctors tell me to, I might never need to have a transplant after all. I've been given a second chance and I'm not going to waste it.

Jenny

Today, two and a half years after he gave up drinking, he is the same Andy he always was, the same Andy I fell in love with all those years ago: sober Andy, the one who laughs more and snaps less than he did when he was drinking.

It's funny, but over all those years I didn't notice the changes in him until he changed back.